MORE FAITHFUL
than we think

LLOYD MACKEY

Foreword by Preston Manning

BayRidge
BOOKS

More Faithful than We Think
Copyright © 2005 Lloyd Mackey
All rights reserved
International Standard Book Number: 1-897213-03-4

Published by:
BayRidge Books
Willard & Associates Consulting Group
1-1295 Wharf Street, Pickering, Ontario, L1W 1A2
Tel: (416) 573-3249 Fax (416) 226-6746
E-mail: info@castlequaybooks.com
www.castlequaybooks.com

Cover Photo: Doug Koop

Library and Archives Canada Cataloguing in Publication
Mackey, Lloyd
 More faithful than we think / Lloyd Mackey.
Based on material previously published in the author's columns:
Capital views, OttawaWatch and Doing politics Christianly.
ISBN 1-897213-03-4

 1. Christianity and politics—Canada. 2. Religious right—Canada. I. Title.
FC635.M32 2005   322'.1'0971   C2005-902622-7

BayRidge
B O O K S

To John and Eleanor Irwin:
You have helped me to understand more clearly
the task of reporting, analyzing and writing
about the things I see, hear and sense.

Table of Contents

Acknowledgements 7
Foreword 9
Introduction:: 9/11 Made a Difference 13

CHAPTER ONE
Across the Spectrum 23

CHAPTER TWO
To Advocate or Legislate 35

CHAPTER THREE
A Sovereigntist in the Camp 53

CHAPTER FOUR
Faith-Based Initiatives: Pre- and Post-Bush 61

CHAPTER FIVE
Pastors and Watchmen 71

CHAPTER SIX
Bobbie: Getting It Together 81

CHAPTER SEVEN
The National Magnet 91

CHAPTER EIGHT
The Care and Feeding of Enemies 109

CHAPTER NINE
Advocacy Here and There 113

CHAPTER TEN
Learning from the Christian Left 127

CHAPTER ELEVEN
Two Funerals: Both Christian, Both Political 137

CHAPTER TWELVE
Anatomy of a Parental Rights Controversy 147

CHAPTER THIRTEEN
Faith's Role in Political Party Strategy 153

CHAPTER FOURTEEN
Jake Epp and Matthew Coon Come 163

CHAPTER FIFTEEN
Out of Service Comes Honour 175

CHAPTER SIXTEEN
One of the Three 185

CHAPTER SEVENTEEN
To Speak or Not to Speak: What Was the Question? 191

CHAPTER EIGHTEEN
Andy Savoy Puts His Ear to the Ground 201

CHAPTER NINETEEN
The Cabinet Minister, the Creator and the Mormons ...205

CHAPTER TWENTY
Responding to the Left and the Right 215

CHAPTER TWENTY-ONE
Resurrecting an Old Blueprint 221

Epilogue 227

Acknowledgements

Much of the content of this book has been drawn from several sources of my own writing during the past six years in Ottawa. In the early years, I wrote a *Passing Scene* column in *Christian News Ottawa*. Much of that material was available to me because of my membership in the Parliamentary Press Gallery. It helped that veteran Gallery member Art Babych was there to give me strategic guidance. At the time, Art covered Parliament Hill for *Canadian Catholic News*, a newsgroup that serves Canada's several regional Catholic newspapers.

When I wrote my letter of application to the Gallery, Art suggested that I indicate I wanted to provide for Protestant publications what he was providing in the Catholic sphere. That proposal was clearly understood by the Gallery executive. The membership gave me the kind of access I needed to the politicians and to resources such as the Parliamentary Library.

For eighteen months, in the period covering the turn of the century, I wrote an e-mail column called *doing politics christianly...*, the title reflecting a phrase coined by Preston Manning. It went to several hundred Christian leaders, influencers and communicators across Canada. I was both encouraged and challenged by the response to it. Especially helpful were the comments that helped me find more leads and ferret out more good stories than I would have been able to find on my own.

After *Christian News Ottawa* rolled over into *ChristianCurrent Ottawa*, I had the responsibility of writing "Capital Views" (later renamed "OttawaWatch") for the inside back page of all *ChristianCurrent* newspapers. That means my material has been finding its way into 1,200 churches across Ontario and, more recently, another 400 in Manitoba. In addition, several Web sites use the column, including canadianchristianity.com, christiancurrent.com, christianity.ca and sundaymagazine.org.

My wife, Edna Mackey, has been the chief bread-winner in our family for many years as I have worked with a number of key Christian journalism and newspaper people in Canada to help build what is now turning into a viable Christian newspaper group. She has worked at several responsible administrative and executive assistant positions at such places as Trinity Western University, Carey Theological College and, at present, in the office of a member of Parliament. Without her administrative skills, I would have found it impossible to handle the Parliament Hill coverage necessary to have gathered the material appearing in this book.

Doug Koop, editorial director of *ChristianWeek* news-paper, Gus Henne and David Visser, marketing director and president, respectively, of Essence Communications Group, have structured my working arrangements in the development of the newspaper group so as to enable my Parliament Hill coverage.

Foreword

Lloyd and Edna Mackey have spent many years living at and observing the interface between faith and politics — Edna in her administrative work for a member of Parliament and various Christian organizations, and Lloyd in his work as a journalist for various Christian and secular publications and as a member of the Parliamentary Press Gallery.

In this book Lloyd revisits many of the events, personalities and stories he has covered from this perspective. These include the memorial services in Canada and the US following the tragedy of September 11, 2001; the efforts of Christian advocacy groups to influence federal policy and legislation on everything from debt forgiveness for poor countries to same-sex marriage; the faith journeys of political activists as diverse as the leaders of the Reform Party and the Canadian Alliance, an American congressman, a Christian sovereigntist, the first Ismaili to sit in the Canadian Parliament, a Conservative cabinet minister and a Pentecostal advisor to Liberal Prime Minister Pierre Trudeau; and the funerals of two Canadian statesmen from very different faith and political backgrounds at opposite ends of the country.

When many of these interview and stories were written, most Canadians were still clinging to the notion that politics and faith could be kept in separate watertight compartments and need not — and should not — "mix." But this position has been made increasingly untenable by the religion polls revealing the depth and breadth of religious persuasion in Canada, the violent intrusion of Islamic extremism on the international political scene and the widespread publicity given to the faith commitments of Tony Blair and George W. Bush and their impact on British and American foreign policy.

The challenge for secular decision makers is now one of understanding how to manage the faith-political interface rather than denying its existence. Likewise the challenge for the leaders and members of faith communities is one of understanding how to live and act wisely and responsibly at that interface. In the light of these challenges, Lloyd Mackey's interviews and stories from the faith-political frontier and his up-to-date commentaries on them are particularly relevant and instructive for the times in which we live.

One further thought occurred to me in reading Lloyd's manuscript and in reflecting on his career as a Christian journalist in the modern media world. The word *media* comes from the same root as the word *mediator* — the word once used by the apostle Paul to describe the reconciling work of Jesus Christ in the world.

The Christian concept of a "media" person is not that of an egocentric champion of either the source or the receiver of a communication; nor is it that of a distant and detached observer. Rather it is that of one who endeavours to enter into the world of both source and receiver and to facilitate an understanding and relationship between the two, based on the communication of truth. Lloyd Mackey's writings and life reflect this desire to facilitate understanding based on truth, between the sources of his stories and those for whom he writes. This book is an eloquent testimony to his personal faith as well as to his journalistic abilities.

PRESTON MANNING
Calgary, Alberta

Introduction

9/11 Made a Difference

September 11, 2001.

During that infamous day and the weeks following, my sense about the relationship between the Christian gospel and the body politic would crystallize immeasurably. And the reason was only partly shaped by the traumatic events that took place at the World Trade Center, at the Pentagon and in a farm field in Pennsylvania.

That morning, I was at my desk, a few hundred feet from the Peace Tower that fronts the Parliament Buildings in Canada's capital, Ottawa. As was often the case, I was browsing the *National Post*, one of Canada's two national daily newspapers. The radio in the background was tuned to CFRA, Ottawa's talk station. Earlier in the day my wife, Edna, and I had shared a reading from a devotional book, *Daily Light*, which began: "Do not conform any longer to the pattern of this world, but be transformed by the renewing of your mind" (Romans 12:2). Reading and pondering a portion of Scripture early in the day and then following it with some attention to the media had become a regular discipline in my quest to "do journalism Christianly" and to cover politics the same way.

Something in the *Post* caught my attention that morning. An editor friend had co-written a piece appearing on the editorial page about the difference between a "sect" and a "church" mindset and the effect of that difference on the way people do politics. I was very struck by the piece and picked up the phone to call my friend so I could tell him how much I appreciated what he was saying. As I was leaving a message, the voice on the radio blurted out that an airplane had just flown into one of the World Trade Center towers at the south tip of Manhattan in New York City.

Soon I was gathered with about twenty other journalists around a couple of television screens in the Parliamentary Press Gallery office, watching the collapse of the World Trade towers.

It was not long before Osama bin Laden began to emerge as the man mainly responsible for 9/11. Along with his name came the frequent reference to his belief, shared by his cohorts in al-Qaeda, that this work of destruction was being done in the name of God.

The *National Post* article to which I referred earlier was a survey of religious historian Richard Niebuhr's exploration of the difference between the mindsets of "church" and "sect." Entitled "Sect and Party," it was co-written by Donald G. Bastian and Gerald Owen. At the time, Bastian was managing editor of Stoddart Publishing and an active Free Methodist layman. Owen was acting books editor at the *Post* and a serious Catholic.

In the piece, they contrasted two models of the relationship between Christianity and culture developed by Niebuhr in his book, *Christ and Culture*. One model is "Christ against culture," often used by people who emphasize that our Christian walk is mainly a "culture war" and that virtually everyone else is against us. The other is "Christ, the transformer of culture." In that model, Bastian and Owen suggested that "if Christ became a man and dwelt among us, perhaps a human being who follows him can become a politician and legislate among us."

The writers used Niebuhr's analogy to explain the religious aspects of the leadership struggle going on in the Canadian Alliance party at the time. More pointedly, they suggested that churches exist within the world system and their leaders see their roles as an influence on that system. In contrast, they implied that sects divide themselves from the world system. By being purists, sectarians hope they can change the system from outside it or, should God permit, actually replace it with a theocracy.

The events of the day have a way of transcending what has happened immediately before, and I suspect that the Bastian–Owen piece has been lost in the dustbins of history because of the attack on the World Trade Center. But I will never forget it. I know what I was thinking about when the attack took place, just as I know where I was when I learned John F. Kennedy had been shot and when King George VI died.

Our *Daily Light* reading that morning was, ironically, a text that is often used by people with a "sect" mindset to encourage a deep cleavage between themselves and all those people in the world system. Apart from that, however, I have often observed that some sectarians lean heavily on the idea that God blesses those who are persecuted. Unethically applied, it permits sectarian leaders to issue damnation on their perceived enemies and then play the persecution card when they receive the desired venomous response. Church leaders who want to exercise political influence, on the other hand, draw sustenance from the biblical directive to be "as shrewd as snakes and as innocent as doves" (Matthew 10:16).

In short, application of that text involves the Christian politician co-opting the assistance of people of integrity within the system who act out of a different set of values. Being as wise as those people yet remaining as innocent, or harmless, as doves is seen by such politicians as the best way to act "Christianly" within the system over the long term.

Two evangelical Christian politicians who take that approach are former Deputy Prime Minister John Manley and Reform Party founder Preston Manning. They both cite nineteenth-century British evangelical statesman William Wilberforce as a formidable precedent. Over the lifetime of his political career, Wilberforce was a key figure in the elimination of the slave trade, but he only saw full success as he approached his own death. Manley and Manning do their politics Christianly, keeping in mind that, like Wilberforce, they are in it for the long haul. They work within a "church" mindset.

Sectarian Christian politicians would prefer to "Christianize" politics to bring in the kingdom, even if that meant they would suffer or die in the process.

One of the main points of this book is to make the case for "doing politics Christianly." I want to do so by telling many of the stories of people who are doing just that, every day, in every party, from various Christian perspectives, with great assistance and to considerable effect.

I want Canadian Christians to know that when they hear their political leaders have turned their backs on God, they are hearing from a sectarian spin on reality. There is some truth to what is said, but it is a tiny sliver of the political and spiritual reality.

I hope that some of the people who read this book will be drawn from what we would generically describe as the evangelical, reformed and charismatic sectors of the Christian church. Out of a population of thirty million-plus Canadians, only about four million are associated to a greater or lesser extent with Christian churches that come from those sectors. More startlingly interesting, fifteen million tell pollsters that their view of Jesus and the Christian gospel is affirming or, at least, sympathetic. They are not the enemy, as the sectarian might tell us: they simply avoid regular attendance at Christian churches. But what they affirm, when asked the right question, is that their relationship with God is predicated on their belief in Jesus, who lived and died and rose again.

My own religio-political pilgrimage has prepared me, in an intriguing way, for covering Ottawa over the past five years and, more relevantly, for writing this book.

The next few paragraphs outline the beginning of my political interest and are excerpted from the introduction to *Like Father, Like Son: Ernest Manning and Preston Manning* (Toronto: ECW Press, 1997), the book I began to write shortly after the death of Ernest C. Manning, Alberta premier from 1943 to 1968 and father to Preston.

Ernest Manning ascended to both the premiership of Alberta and the radio pulpit of Canada's national Back to the Bible Hour *in 1943, at the age of thirty-four. It had been just a year since his wife, Muriel, had given birth to Preston, the second of their two sons.*

17

Over the mountains and across Georgia Strait, in Victoria, a boy of three was completely unaware of those seemingly far-off events. Within a decade, though, I was to undergo my political coming of age.

My father was a firefighter and my mother was a home-maker. I had a brother a tad younger than Preston Manning and a sister who was born in 1949. Our parents were devout members of Oaklands Gospel Hall, part of a loosely-knit group of churches collectively nicknamed the Christian Brethren or Plymouth Brethren. Faith, not politics, was their main agenda.

Around 1951, having been given the family five-tube table radio after my parents splurged on a new Chisholm radio-phonograph, I began listening on Sunday afternoons to some of the radio preachers whose names were sometimes mentioned in church. Most of them, such as Billy Graham, Charles E. Fuller, Walter Maier and Myron F. Boyd, were American. But one afternoon, I discovered that there was a Canadian in the crowd – no less than the premier of Alberta, Ernest C. Manning.

A few months later, having been taught tithing – giving ten percent of my earnings to God – I sent $1.23 from my Victoria Times *paper route to the premier. A kindly letter arrived at our home just days later, thanking me for the money and quoting from Ecclesiastes 11:1, which reads "Cast your bread upon the waters, for after many days you will find it again."*

The years passed and I grew to young manhood, attending Bible college, serving short pastoral internships and shifting into journalism. In 1979, I was assigned by Decision, *the magazine published by Billy Graham, to interview Manning, who was now a senator. He had accepted the appointment of honorary chair of a Billy Graham mission a few months later in Edmonton.*

After one of the Graham meetings, the senator intro-duced me to Preston. We kept in touch. Then, in 1986, during a lunch meeting, Preston pulled some papers out of his briefcase and showed them to me. The papers described plans for a new political party called Reform. Three years later, I began a two-year contract stint as editor of the party's newspaper, The Reformer.

That, then, was part of the story that brought me to writing what appears on these pages.

When I did that interview with Preston's father for *Decision*, I had been editor of *The Chilliwack Progress* for almost six years. The *Progress* was firmly planted in the Fraser Valley Bible belt yet was, as a good community newspaper should be, slightly aloof from it. (The Fraser Valley federal riding has for the most part elected evan-gelical Christian members of Parliament over the past thirty years, with the political stripes ranging from Social Credit to Conservative to Reform to Alliance. That story will be a part of one of the chapters in this book.)

Editing and writing for the community's leading news-paper gave me a perspective on the in-working of a range of Christian values. In the early seventies, I covered the rise of the short-lived NDP government under Dave Barrett. He was a self-declared agnostic but was shaped by both Baptist clergyman and NDP founder Tommy Douglas's social gospel and an education in similar Catholic Jesuitical philosophy as that espoused by Pierre Elliott Trudeau.

In the mid-seventies, I was a staff writer for the *United Church Observer* before returning to *The Chilliwack Progress*, where I had begun my journalism career. The *Observer* experience helped round out my understanding of the left-liberal approach to the social gospel. The United Church was often referred to as "the NDP at prayer." Like most truisms, it had enough truth to prevent it from being a complete misquote.

The next step in my religio-political interfacing came in the early eighties, coincidental with my completing MBA studies at Simon Fraser University. That was when I was involved in the founding of what is now *BC Christian News*, a monthly tabloid distributed in 1,000 BC churches. Periodically, my interest in the development of local and regional Christian newspapers took me to central Canada to "spy out the land" and to assist in the development of several such journals.

Then, in 1998, during the run-up to a Billy Graham mission in Ottawa, Edna and I moved to the national capital, where I became engaged in the development of a newspaper called *Christian News Ottawa*. In 2002, it morphed into *ChristianCurrent Ottawa*, part of a newspaper group developed in a strategic alliance with a national paper called *ChristianWeek*. The Ottawa move gave me a new observation perch, that of the Parliamentary Press Gallery.

I spent enough time in Ontario to realize that the interfacing of faith and politics was a little more complex than it was in the western provinces. The strong historic influence of both mainstream Protestantism and Catholicism created different kinds of linkages than those I had found in western Canada. It likely explained why, despite having a national Christian radio ministry, Ernest Manning never ventured into federal elected politics. And it could be what caused his son's move toward the prime ministership to falter.

That Pierre Trudeau appointed the senior Manning to the senate, where he laboured quietly and prodigiously for some thirteen years, was a bit of a conundrum, because the two men were quite different in both philosophy and style. Still, Trudeau set an example for what could be a good move by whoever is prime minister when this book makes it to print. He could appoint Preston Manning to the upper chamber, where he would provide a form of senior statesmanship that would incorporate both his faith and his political values. In that way, he would have a decade and a half to be Canada's twenty-first-century Wilberforce, simply by doing politics Christianly.

The possibility of such a senatorial appointment has likely faded recently, with the establishment of a think-tank known as the Manning Centre for Building Democracy.

I wrap up my introduction to this book with that observation because, as we embark on the chapters that follow, we will meet many people who have all kinds of ways to bring Christian values to bear on public policy and the political process.

As stated earlier, it was Preston Manning who coined the phrase "doing politics Christianly," back when he was a member of the board of governors at Regent College, an evangelical graduate school at the University of British Columbia. He did so when the Reform party was still a gleam in his eye. And, in the intervening twenty years, he has, for the most part, successfully practised what he preached.

My suggestion has been that, after putting together the Canadian Alliance and failing to win its leadership, he moved into the "Jimmy Carter" phase of his life. Like the former United States president, Manning junior used high office as a stepping stone to something more significant. That is, he has been able to apply the values of Christian reconciliation to the political process in a way that is somewhat apart from the hurly-burly of our adversarial political system.

In the following chapters, I share articles I have written for the "doing politics christianly…," "OttawaWatch" and "Capital Views" columns. They have been slightly altered so as to make them appropriate for this book, also keeping in mind that readers may not have read previous articles and that the material is dated.

Chapter One

Across the Spectrum

At the outset, I would like to relate to my fellow evangelical, reformed or charismatic brothers and sisters about what happens right across the Christian spectrum with respect to the faith/politics dynamic. It involves not only "seeing ourselves as others see us" but unpacking many of the parallel activities that evangelicals might not recognize as "doing politics Christianly." There is less of a gap between politics and faith than we think, and both conservative and liberal Christians will see that each side's approach is not so far off from the other.

To Pray or Not to Pray

US President George W. Bush quoted the Bible when he spoke at a National Cathedral service in memory of those who died in the September 11 attack on the World Trade Center and the Pentagon.

His approach was in sharp contrast to Prime Minister Jean Chrétien's studied avoidance of any deity-associated language during his address to a crowd of 100,000 at a Parliament Hill event two days later, on September 14.

That contrast subsequently drew many responses from a whole range of people, many of whom wondered why an open show of faith should be so much more difficult for Canadian leaders than for their American counterparts.

During the Washington service, Bush quoted Romans 8:38,39, which reads, "For I am convinced that neither death nor life, neither angels nor demons, neither the present nor the future, nor any powers, neither height nor depth, nor anything else in all creation, will be able to separate us from the love of God."

Chrétien, however, kept his language neutral. He did use the theologically-loaded phrase *saving grace,* but in a secular context, suggesting that such grace was reflected in "humanity" and "decency." The phrase is usually used by Christians to describe a sovereign God's reaching out to his creation.

But, just in case no one noticed, President Bush used a little diplomacy to ensure that his quoting from a Christian epistle would not prove offensive to either Jews or Muslims or, for that matter, any other followers of a monotheistic religion. He stopped the Romans 8:39 reference at "the love of God." He left out "that is in Christ Jesus our Lord."

His was the "Jesus understood" approach. Political leaders and even some clergypersons use it on public occasions to play down any sense that they want to use a non-sectarian setting to proselytize. The popular television show *Touched by an Angel* uses it to communicate its obviously Christian values through the television medium without being harassed by those civil liberties types who see a Jesus freak behind every lamppost.

The argument is that people who have some knowledge of Jesus and the gospel will know where to insert his name and will thus be able to receive the spiritual sustenance that the Scripture references and prayers are intended to provide.

Former federal minister David Kilgour, for some years responsible for Latin American and African affairs, a sometime constitutional lawyer and one of the cabinet's most prolific Christian spokespersons, said he is mystified by the contrast between the Bush and Chrétien approaches. "The American constitution emphatically separates church and state; ours is virtually silent, yet American leaders often speak as though there is no separation. But a lot of [Canadian] people think [our leaders] keep the separation clear."

Kilgour, along with Heritage Minister Sheila Copps, played a key role in facilitating two memorial services on the Hill in the days following the tragedy. One, an interdenominational service, drew twenty MPs on September 18. Its high point was the group's unaccompanied singing in four-part harmony of "Amazing Grace" and "What a Friend We Have in Jesus."

The next day, an interfaith event brought an attendance of 300 politicians and diplomats, among them some seventy MPs, including several senior cabinet ministers and party leaders.

For their own parts, Canada's head of government and head of state did their religious "thing" away from the public glare of the big Hill event. Chrétien attended a memorial mass at nearby Notre Dame Cathedral with his wife, Aline, just moments after the thousands dispersed from the Parliament Buildings' lawn. Art Babych, writing at the time for *Canadian Catholic News*, recounted that Ottawa Archbishop Marcel Gervais, in effect, told the PM to "be there!"

On the Sunday afternoon following, Governor General Adrienne Clarkson and her consort, John Ralston Saul, took in an interfaith service at Christ Church Cathedral. Her aides reminded the media people that Her Excellency is a practising Anglican whose home parish is St. Bartholomew's, just across the road from Rideau Hall. At both the Anglican service and the Hill interfaith event, Christian, Jewish, First Nations, Hindu, Sikh and Muslim clergy offered prayers.

However, it was the prime minister's decision to avoid the uttering of prayers on the Hill that drew the ire of, or at least surprise from, many people who look for spiritual guidance from temporal leaders. Some surprise came from Rahim Jaffer, an Edmonton Alliance MP and the only Muslim in the House of Commons.

Jaffer, a member of the relatively liberal Ismaili form of Islam led by the Aga Khan, said he would like to have seen the prime minister act sooner to encourage Canadians to make prayer a part of their handling of the terror. But he was pleased that Chrétien visited an Ottawa mosque on the afternoon of September 21. A fairly active Muslim who tries to attend prayers most Fridays, Jaffer is troubled about some of the attacks by non-Muslims on people of obvious Arab origins.

However, asked if he, as the only Muslim in the Commons, is ever a target for proselytizing by Christian MPs or party supporters, Jaffer seemed surprised by the question. He quickly answered "No," suggesting that he has found most Christians he knows to be extending and interested in understanding his faith. (It was a good question to ask him, knowing that at least one-third of the Canadian Alliance caucus, to which he belonged, were evangelical Christians who are supposed to be committed to converting other people to Christ.)

Meanwhile, an American Christian rightist had come in for some cautious criticism from a former Ottawa clergyman who now works in New York City. Christian-right leader Jerry Falwell was quoted in the September 15 *Globe and Mail*, describing the New York and Washington destruction as God's retribution for sinful behaviour. He specifically singled out civil liberties groups, abortionists, feminists, gays and lesbians as those who "helped this happen." Hours later, he withdrew and apologized for the statement, after a public dressing-down from President Bush.

One person who disagreed with Falwell's original assertion was David Epstein, senior minister at New York's Calvary Baptist Church. (For several years, he held the same post at Ottawa's Metropolitan Bible Church, a large downtown congregation.)

Epstein's theology and moral teachings are similar to Falwell's, but his 1,300-strong church is in the heart of the theatre district and also has a strong ministry to homosexuals. He told me he was prepared to publicly disclaim the Falwell statements. In his mind, every part of American society could stand spiritual awakening. It is unnecessarily combative, and perhaps inaccurate, to single out specific groups for attention, he suggested.

Calvary Baptist's story was just one of thousands illustrating faith in action post 9/11. The church is located about four miles north of "ground zero." During those days when the transportation systems were down, hundreds of people walking in the only direction they could, disoriented and dazed, stopped off at the church for help. Dozens of church volunteers and staffers offered practical help and counselling. People needed money, changes of clothes, showers and, often, more.

Calvary Baptist was not alone. Epstein spoke of other churches in the community with which they work closely, among them Fifth Avenue Presbyterian, a congregation that captured the attention of key Liberal strategist and former Trudeau cabinet minister David Smith.

Smith, a Baptist and prominent Toronto lawyer, maintains close familial and spiritual ties with two Pentecostal minister brothers. As it happens, he was in Manhattan and watched a Fifth Avenue Presbyterian memorial service on television. He unabashedly told me that the choir rendered the old spiritual "My Lord, what a morning, when the sun refused to shine" with nary a "dry eye in the crowd."

As to advice for the PM and "Brother Manley," as he informally described the devoutly Presbyterian foreign affairs minister, Smith cautiously suggested "wisdom, common sense and strategic thinking in the days ahead, with peace always being our foremost goal." He cited James 4:17,18 to plead his case.

The dust-up over prayer provided some basis for parliamentary debate. Reform party founder Preston Manning, who has an uncanny way of translating Christianese into sage counsel, suggested that "our nations, particularly in times of war and disaster, have sought deliverance from evil and the strength to do good through faith in the justice and grace of God."

Then he slid a little prayer into the Hansard House of Commons record (September 17, 2001). He requested that "the tragedy of September 11, 2001 will lead…our spiritual leaders [to] speak the truth in love or not at all; and that our political leaders will be given the wisdom to fashion our response to terrorism and its roots in the light of the moral imperatives which this tragedy illuminates."

Manning conceded that Canadian politicians seem shy about "publicly embracing the spiritual realities of life." He said, "In our secular and pluralistic society, we seem incapable of even discussing, let alone taking direction from, our spiritual heritage or clear standards of right and wrong based upon it. We are too much fearful of being misunderstood and thereby dividing rather than uniting our people."

The Alliance communications office let it be known later that Manning was quoting from a Civil War prayer uttered by Abraham Lincoln.

However, there was more. On September 29, I filed "doing politics christianly…" #42, an account of two very different prayer meetings that had taken place on the Hill subsequent to 9/11.

A Tale of Two Prayer Meetings

Last week, I made mention of two Parliament Hill memorial services for the victims of the September 11 attack. One, an interfaith service, drew 300 politicians and diplomats, including about seventy members of Parliament. It received wide television coverage. The other, billed as an "interdenominational service," was specifically Christian in nature. It drew twenty MPs plus a handful of aides. There were no cameras there and only one person from the press gallery – your humble scribe.

The interfaith service was a good event. It took place under the patronage of Heritage Minister Sheila Copps and Latin America/Africa Secretary of State David Kilgour. The chair was John McKay, Liberal MP for Scarborough East and chair of the National Prayer Breakfast.

I always appreciate interfaith services, even with my evangelical perspective and my congenial acquiescence to Jesus' assertion that "I am the way, the truth and the life: No one comes to the Father but by me" (John 14:6). This service was important to the politicians and those who work with them because it provided the opportunity for them to hear, with good will, the prayers offered by people of several faiths.

It was particularly essential at that point to hear the praying of Islamic leaders and to allow Islamic, Jewish and Christian politicians to reflect on the fact that they are not enemies.

Further, the apparent ban on the mentioning of the name of Jesus, which gained notoriety during the Swissair crash memorial service at Peggy's Cove three years ago, was not in evidence. Christian clergy had just as much right to invoke their deity's name as anyone else had.

Although the prime minister was not present, several senior cabinet ministers were, as were most of the other party leaders.

There was a good deal of healing during that service. It was not only worthwhile but essential to the spiritual health of more than a few Canadian leaders. The other, smaller, service is the one I would like to spend a bit of time analyzing. For me, its spiritual and emotional impact was considerable. And there were underlying reasons. It was held in the Sean O'Sullivan Room, a small meditation place in the East Block on Parliament Hill. The room is named for a Conservative MP who became a Catholic priest and then died of cancer before he reached forty.

For me, the high points of that service were the group singing of "What a Friend We Have in Jesus" and "Amazing Grace," Reed Elley's prayer and the personal stories told by Preston Manning and Jerry Sherman.

And the other thing: seated in close quarters were Liberal, Alliance and Progressive Conservative/Democratic Reform members of Parliament, all serious Christian believers and all experiencing their own spiritual struggles and tensions growing out of leadership issues in their particular political parties. Chuck Strahl, deputy leader of the PC-DR, was called on to lead the singing. Strong and rich of voice and confident in his public presentation, Strahl is semi-shy and self-effacing when involved in a task such as this. He grinned almost sheepishly and said, "If I am going to lead, I will need some help." And help they did. The harmony would have done the Gaithers proud, and the healing touch of congregational singing was evident.

The two stories during the service brought the September 11 events close to home for those who were present.

Preston Manning, who was there with his wife, Sandra, was called on for a Scripture reading because the previously-planned MP reader couldn't get there. Manning prefaced the reading with a simple account of the hour of anxiety they experienced after the blast. One of their daughters, Mary Joy, works in the Manhattan financial district. The anxiety ended when she called them, reporting that she was alive and well.

Jerry Sherman's story was quite dramatic. Sherman heads the Christian Embassy, a Campus Crusade ministry that works with politicians and diplomats in Ottawa. He began the homily with his recounting of his own activities on the morning of September 11.

He was flying over the World Trade Center twin towers early that morning, before landing and heading for a prayer breakfast at the United Nations. Bright blue sky and glassy, calm waters surrounded Manhattan, and he thought to himself: "How peaceful."

News of the attack awaited the prayer breakfast attendees as they emerged from their session at about 10 a.m. The day became a blur.

Very quickly, Sherman moved from praying with UN officials to handing out bottled water, Salvation-Army style, at 2nd and 52nd, where thousands of people were heading north on foot from ground zero.

Art Hanger had just returned to the main Alliance caucus from the DR (which had been formed to accomodate Alliance MPs dissenting from Stockwell Day's leadership). Hanger was scheduled to deliver the main prayer at the O'Sullivan Room service. He stood down to Reed Elley, who was pastor of First Baptist Church, Nanaimo, before entering politics.

Take my word for it. Elley is a man of God – or, at least, a godly man. His profile is not high on the House floor. But he is a pastor par excellence, and he moved the gathering into the presence of God and a deep awareness of what forgiveness and compassion will come to mean in the Christian community in the weeks and months to come.

It was intriguing to see Manning and Elley in the same room, keeping in mind the remarks US Christian-right leader Jerry Falwell uttered – then withdrew – about what he believed to be the role of the gay community in triggering God's judgment on America.

Many Christians trace Manning's fall from grace with some of the evangelical Christian community to his dressing-

down of two of his MPs who made disparaging remarks about gays some months before the 1997 election. One of the MPs did not run again, and the person who ran for that seat was Elley.

That the Reform founder could attract someone like Elley to run for office after allegedly losing favour with some evangelicals is a conundrum worth pondering. Part of the answer is that Christian people imbued with the grace of God are able to exercise spiritual leadership and, at the same time, treat with respect and care those who differ from themselves morally and spiritually.

Elley's strength that day was in exercising his pastoral gifts. It was good of Hanger to step aside. In so doing, he showed the kind of spiritual discernment and respect for order that has marked his careers as MP and, before that, RCMP officer.

Just a little task for a leisure moment: the Scriptures read at the O'Sullivan Room service were Psalm 96, Romans 8:31–39 and John 20:19–26. A reading of them will help plug you into what made that service meaningful for those who were there.

For people who like their stories told chronologically, 9/11 calls for a bending of the rules.

Read on, and you will learn of some of the behind-the-scenes activities that bring influence to bear on politicians. Some of these activities happen all across the nation; others take place on the Hill itself.

Chapter Two

To Advocate or Legislate

Christians have access to the political process in Ottawa through many channels. In this chapter, we will take a look at the roles of advocacy groups, special caucuses and round tables.

Each month, half a dozen distributors deliver *ChristianCurrent Ottawa* to some 400 churches and other places where Christians are likely to be found. I have the delivery job for Centretown Ottawa, close to the Parliament Buildings, for myself. It gives me a chance to see the people involved in several Christian organizations whose offices are there mainly because they want to keep close contact with the politicians and bureaucrats. I call it my "walking route," because it would be more difficult to drive to the offices than to take a bundle of papers under my arm and drop a few off at each stop.

These are the names of the organizations on my route — plus a brief comment about each:

- *Evangelical Fellowship of Canada.* This is where EFC president Bruce Clemenger and legal counsel Janet Epp Buckingham prepare briefs for parliamentary committees and review new legislation for its possible impact on the 1.5 million people whose denominations are members of the fellowship. This "umbrella group" is one of three representing a broad cross-section of three sectors of Canadian Christendom. The other two are the Canadian Council of Churches and Canadian Conference of Catholic Bishops. Sometimes the EFC prepares joint briefs with the other two groups; on other occasions they may consult but each group brings forward its own perspective. The leaders of the three see their respective roles on this level as complementary, rather than competitive or conflicting.

- *Laurentian Leadership Centre.* This fine old mansion houses the Ottawa presence of Trinity Western University. Here, twenty-five or so third- and fourth-year international relations, political science and communications students from the BC-based Christian university spend one semester being taught in the ways of political Ottawa and interning in the offices of cabinet ministers, members of Parliament, government agencies and Hill media. The dream of Don Page, who took on a senior leadership role at TWU twenty years ago after being a senior policy advisor for several foreign affairs ministers, the centre is directed by Paul Wilson, former research director for the official opposition.

- *Initiatives for Change.* The Ottawa office of this organization, formerly known as Moral Re-Armament, is run by Richard Weeks. IFC is established on an approach to political morality based on biblical Christianity, although its current work internationally reflects the compatible values of a number of world religions.

- *Christian Embassy.* This is a ministry of Campus Crusade for Christ. Director Jerry Sherman works closely with members of Parliament, senators and diplomats in helping them to commit to and understand the Christian gospel. The embassy's work includes arranging weekly Bible studies with MPs and senators, providing opportunities for diplomats to meet Canadian leaders in faith-based settings and arranging overseas trips for politicians wanting to observe the activity of other nations from a Christian perspective.

- *Mennonite Central Committee.* Bill Janzen directs this office, which brings the concerns of some 250,000 Canadian Mennonites to the Hill. MCC runs a highly effective relief and development agency well regarded throughout the world. Part of Janzen's work is to liaise with CIDA (Canadian International Development Agency), which, among other things, helps to fund the development work of many NGOs (non-government organizations), a number of which, like MCC, are Christian based.

- *Salvation Army.* Dani Shaw, a lawyer who previously worked with the Evangelical Fellowship, is the Salvation Army's parliamentary liaison. The SA, with its long and broad experience in Christian-based social service and action, is in an excellent position to provide good advice on social policy issues to politicians and bureaucrats.

- *Sean O'Sullivan Room.* This is not an agency but a quiet place of meditation within the parliamentary precinct. Once a week, ten to twenty-five support staffers from the Hill meet for Bible study. They are linked with a broader organization known as the Public Service

Christian Fellowship, which has a few dozen small study groups in various government departments. The room is named for a Catholic who, in his twenties, was a member of Parliament politically mentored by John Diefenbaker, a colourful Baptist who was prime minister from 1957 to 1963. O'Sullivan left politics to become a priest. In that capacity, he had a strong desire to recruit others into the priesthood and designed a billboard campaign depicting Jesus hanging on the cross. The caption for the display was "Dare to be a Priest like me." The theology behind it was understandably more Catholic than Baptist, but those who know claim that it served the campaign's purpose effectively. O'Sullivan's full life was cut off by leukemia before he was forty.

- *Church Council for Justice and Corrections*. The leadership team in this office keeps in touch with politicians and bureaucrats with faith-based input on justice and corrections issues. It draws its strongest support from liberal-leaning churches as well as from Mennonites, who are steeped in the teachings of Christian pacifism. Much of its work has focused in recent years on helping Hill people understand the concept of restorative justice as an alternative to traditional correctional approaches. For some years Rick Prashaw handled CCJC communications, before taking on a similar role for Catholic NDP MP Tony Martin.

These small but strategically significant offices reflect a variety of Christian influences around the Hill. They are representative of a myriad of Christian clusters throughout Canada. If politics is the reconciling of conflicting interests, then these organizations and many others, often described as advocacy groups, help bring a range of viewpoints to the Hill that politicians can process.

In the next three "doing politics christianly..." pieces, we will look at the different ways in which these groups gather their support, then bring it to Ottawa. In December of 2000, I wrote "doing politics christianly..." #3 about the community-impact seminars that were developed across the country in the early nineties and the way in which they eventually brought issues to focus in Ottawa.

WHY THE IMPACT?

Remember the community-impact seminars that proliferated across western and, to a lesser extent, central Canada during the early nineties? They were mostly sponsored by Focus on the Family Canada. Before that, Tyndale University College and Seminary president Brian Stiller, who was the Evangelical Fellowship of Canada president at the time, was taking his Understanding our Times seminars across Canada.

More recently, the Canadian Ecumenical Jubilee Initiative has used similar methods to educate Christian people about world poverty and debt issues. The initiative has drawn support from the Canadian Conference of Catholic Bishops and officialdom in mainline Protestant denominations. Its keenest advocates in the evangelical community have been World Vision Canada and Citizens for Public Justice.

There are similarities and differences in these three approaches to Christian political action. The similarities are reflected in the fact that all three have used biblical bases for developing their ideas and proceed from there to equip Christian people to bring these ideas to bear on the body politic.

All three worked with ministers, churches and other clusters of Christians, encouraging them to live out their Christianity by persuading communities and their leaders to listen and act on what they had to say. Often, they had clear ideas about the kinds of political action they hoped their targets would take.

There is demonstrable evidence that all three have recently left their impact, directly and otherwise, on the federal political scene.

Their differences reflect the particular choice of biblical concepts that each approach has chosen to highlight and the segments of Christendom that they targeted.

The community impact seminars chose the parts of the Bible that emphasize pro-life and pro-family messages. Usually one day in length, a typical seminar, under skilled leadership, took the 100 or more attendees through a process that left them with definite ideas about which biblical issues in particular required action. The underlying assumption was that there were forces in the nation that were trying to undermine traditional family and life values and that some kind of Christian-based "community impact" was needed to counter those forces.

Brian Stiller's seminars attempted to help Christians, in the words of Scripture, to "understand the times" so they could work toward political action that would be relevant to the politicians who were prepared to listen to them. Indeed, during his tenure as EFC president, the groundwork was laid for a strong official evangelical presence in Ottawa that has persistently attempted to bring biblical perspectives to bear on a range of social and economic issues. It worked hard to see that a traditional definition of marriage was maintained in Bill C-23, the act that introduced a range of new benefits to same-sex couples. Its impact, along with that of others,

bore some fruit in the Liberal, Reform and Conservative cau-
cuses during the C-23 debate in the spring of 2000.

World Vision utilized many of the Jubilee concepts in
its popular Thirty Hour Famines to help young participants
understand the stated reasons that wealthy countries such as
Canada needed to reduce what the poorest nations owed
them. It was the debt, they maintained, that ate up the money
that otherwise could be diverted to poverty alleviation and
education programs that would give a fighting chance to the
next generation. Role playing, animation and other aware-
ness-raising and educational techniques were used to while
away the famine hours productively.

The fact is that much of the effectiveness of the three
groups has been to reinforce the particular ideologies of the var-
ious political parties and certain segments within the parties.

Whether they realized it or not, many of the people
encouraging the community impact seminars were laying
the groundwork for serious biblical considerations among
members of the Mulroney Tory caucus and, later, the
Manning Reformers. Both those parties had — and still
have — people who were well placed to encourage evangelical
Christian involvement in their particular interests. They
were good at saying: "We need you and your biblical per-
spective in the political process. Come join us and let us
work with you."

When the Canadian Alliance came on the scene, that
process was furthered, thus the reason faith became some-
thing to talk about during the last election campaign.

The "last election campaign" was that held in
November 2000. Some of the campaign issues revolved
around how much party leaders should let religious faith
or theology influence the way they do politics.

Stiller's emphases spilled further across the political boundaries. His influence has been as strong in Ontario as in the west. Thus, many of the Christians who might vote Alliance if they lived in the west cast their ballots for the federal Liberals. Not that Stiller told them to; rather, there were influencers in the Liberal camp that could persuade Ontario evangelicals that the Liberals have enough "social conservatives" in their ranks to protect their interests.

And the Jubilee people? They always have a hearing with the "social gospel" sector of the NDP, but that does not carry them too far these days. More significantly, they have been successful in getting the ear, and the action, of Finance Minister Paul Martin, a somewhat-conservative type of Liberal who might well have been Tory or CA if he had come out of Alberta rather than Ontario and Quebec.

Martin, after all, has used a modified form of fiscal conservatism to get our own debt down, then to embark on a tax reduction program. Now, he can afford to listen to those in the Christian left who have recovered the biblical concept of debt forgiveness and applied it in a global perspective. It should not go unnoticed that, in pleading for debt forgiveness, social gospel people are tacitly accepting what many on the left tend to play down: that debt hurts people.

There are many interesting political bedfellows in and around the Hill. Some of them are Christians, among them those who would view their fellow believers in other ideological camps as political heretics. The adage that "politics is the reconciling of conflicting interests" has something biblical to say about this whole process.

In "doing politics christianly…"#19, written April 21, 2001, I spoke of the Christian left-leaning advocacy approach to political and international economics articulated by former United Church moderator Robert Smith, one of the great recent orators in his denomination.

For evangelical Christians, the value in taking a look at an approach such as Robert Smith's is to take note of the parallel strategies that become a part of the evangelical, or at least faith-based social conservative, way of doing things when advocating for pro-life and pro-family causes.

THE MISERY OF MY PEOPLE...

I was tempted to use the headline: "A 'monstrous fraud' against my people..." After all, those were the words used by Robert Smith. He was identifying what, to him, is a fraud perpetrated by Canada, the United States and Mexico through the exercise of free trade.

As I heard Smith mouth the words, I said to myself, "There is a good headline grabber. Let's see how it plays in tomorrow's Globe and Mail."

The Globe did get "monstrous fraud" into the sub-head, missing the story's main caption only because "monstrous" was likely too long to fit.

Robert Smith is one of Canada's finest preachers in the liberal-left tradition. He has the proverbial passion and piercing stare of an Old Testament prophet.

A former United Church moderator, Smith filled the prestigious pulpit of Shaughnessy Heights United Church in Vancouver for over a decade before becoming superintendent of First United Church, a few miles to the northeast and, in cultural terms, a million light-years away.

But that is Smith's way. He adheres rigidly to the social gospel's doctrine of God's "preferential option for the poor."

He enunciated that doctrine in the courts of the rich at Shaughnessy Heights. His congregants listened to his elo-quence and acted on it because they respected him as a pastor. Then, at First United in the downtown East Side, he was on the front lines in the lowest-income community in Canada.

Fast forward, now, to this past Thursday, April 19, 2001, when Robert Smith and some fellow church leaders staged a press conference on Parliament Hill. Their visit coincided with the arrival in town of Vicente Fox, the new president of Mexico. The clerics were meeting later in the day with Fox to tell him they believe the North American Free Trade Agreement (NAFTA) is hurting Mexico's poor.

The sessions with the press and Fox were put together by Kathy Price, communication officer for the Inter-Church Committee on Human Rights in Latin America (ICHLA), a group with ties to the Canadian Council of Churches and Canadian Conference of Catholic Bishops.

Invoking the "monstrous fraud" phrase, Smith told the story of the border city of Ciudad Juarez, home to 397 maquila factories employing 281,000 workers who assemble electronics products and car parts for export to the United States and Canada. In brief, his point was that in this city, whose free trade zone status predates NAFTA by twenty-five years, it took three factory jobs to maintain one family in a cardboard shack. (Fox counters that it takes time for the ben-efits of free trade to permeate a whole community.)

But where was the biblical approach in all this?

For that, we go back to my headline.

At the above-mentioned press conference, ICHLA released a letter that five church leaders, including Smith, had written to Prime Minister Jean Chrétien, host of this weekend's Summit of the Americas in Quebec City. In that letter, the clerics spoke of the "soul-wrenching human suffering we witnessed during a fact-finding visit to Mexico just two weeks ago – suffering that evoked for all of us God's call to Moses: 'I have seen the misery of my people...I have heard their cry' (Exodus 3:7)."

I had a different Mexico-related question for the group.

A few years before, while covering a North America Synod meeting of the Reformed Church of America (RCA), whose two most famous preachers are Robert Schuller and the late Norman Vincent Peale, I learned about one-half million Presbyterian people in the Chiapas region of Mexico whose Christian commitment had sprung from a remarkable spiritual revival several decades ago.

The region was in the news at the time of that synod because of the Chiapas rebellion, which pitted insurgents against the then-failing Mexican government. The RCA people explained that there was a sub-struggle within the rebellion that was generating considerable hardship among the Presbyterians at the hands of the dominant Catholic group.

At this week's press conference, I asked what church leaders had to say about this issue.

Kathy Price responded that the Chiapas situation had, indeed, been portrayed as a religious struggle. But she maintained that the real story was more about economics and differing views on property rights. She claimed that much reconciliation has occurred between the struggling religious groups.

All of the above is a snapshot of one of the two Christian "solitudes" that periodically surface on the Hill. This is the "social justice" solitude, and its counterpoint is the "social conservative" perspective; the latter advocates for pro-life and pro-family perspectives.

45

Robert Smith can be just as biblically eloquent as Roy Byer, a strong social conservative advocate and a Victory Church pastor from Edmonton and former president of the Canada Family Action Coalition. They would see each other as enemies or, at least, as keen competitors. They would maintain quite different perspectives on what is biblical truth and would see their own particular takes on truth as essential to the betterment of society.

I talk about this as an evangelical Christian, writing mostly to fellow evangelicals, in an effort to keep things in perspective. There are likely about 70 to 100 MPs who would take what Robert Smith says seriously and a similar number who would listen with care to Roy Byer. The rest will listen to neither or, if they are smart, both.

Many evangelicals will not agree with what Smith has to say about economics and globalization. But we do well to listen carefully, because the issues he raises are relevant and their resolution requires leadership initiative – albeit possibly different than what Smith would advocate. Those evangelicals who lean more toward Smith's perspective should not ignore Byer's viewpoint. CFAC often does good research into issues that no one else will touch – and somebody has to.

This next piece is an example of the work that parliamentary "round tables" can do to bring a strong focus to bear on one particular issue. One or two members of Parliament from any party can undertake a round table. Whatever permission is necessary comes from the speaker's office together with the necessary arrangements regarding the procuring of an assembly room, publicizing of the event to all MPs and the retaining of expert resource people who can bring new information about the issue to the table.

Round tables are generally low-key. Few reporters cover them, although they are open to the media. Because there is little coverage, politicians will often speak forthrightly, recognizing that they will not likely garner sensational headlines from what they say in relative obscurity.

This particular piece was written April 16, 2002, not long after the Supreme Court of Canada brought down its decision in the John Robin Sharpe child porn case.

ROUND TABLE: SHARPE CORNERS

The "artistic merit" issue surrounding the John Robin Sharpe case was the subject of some well-publicized responses around Ottawa this past week.

In the process, there was an almost seamless move from advocacy to activism that went right into the heart of every political party represented in the House of Commons.

It all began Thursday, April 11, with a Parliament Buildings press conference spurred by an anti-child-pornography campaign launched the same day by Focus on the Family Canada. That event led almost directly to an all-party round table five days later, facilitated by Liberal MP Dan McTeague.

The Focus campaign emerged as a response to the early April British Columbia Supreme Court decision in which Justice Duncan Shaw ruled that John Robin Sharpe could not be convicted for having written stories describing admittedly violent and sadistic sex acts between adults and children. Justice Shaw argued that there was "some artistic merit" in the writings.

He had also drawn from a Supreme Court of Canada decision a few months earlier, again focused on Sharpe's activities. He noted that the high court delineated between sexually explicit child-related materials that use real children in their production and those that are created from the author's imagination.

Sharpe is a former town planner who has gained national attention through his strong advocacy of adult-child sex. That attention has been heightened through three court cases over the past two years, which have focused on his views and activities.

Darrel Reid, then Focus Canada's president, facilitated the press conference that preceded the round table. Reid, in one of his earlier roles, was chief of staff in the Official Opposition office, three floors above where this event took place.

At the outset, Reid explained that it was Focus Canada's intention to raise awareness of the BC decision and spur action that would hopefully lead to its nullification, either through further court action or a parliamentary initiative. He pointed out that a national newspaper and radio campaign had begun that morning.

However, as an experienced strategist, Reid saw to it that the focus of the press conference was the choice of politicians who addressed the tiny group of assembled media.

They were:

- *Victor Toews (pronounced Taves), Canadian Alliance justice critic and respected former attorney-general of Manitoba.*
- *Elsie Wayne, "den mother" of the Progressive Conservative caucus, who could always be expected to speak out on pro-family issues.*
- *Dan McTeague, a suburban Toronto Liberal MP who often speaks for pro-life and pro-family issues – and is respected in his caucus for doing so.*

Joining the group at his own request was Grant Hill, a recent CA leadership candidate. He was there to point out that newly-elected CA leader Stephen Harper was prepared to lend the party's endorsement to the Focus Canada campaign.

An interesting—and not irrelevant—sidelight is the denominational affiliation of each of the above named: Toews (Mennonite Brethren), Wayne (Baptist), McTeague (Catholic), Hill (Mormon) and Harper (Christian and Missionary Alliance).

Hill's appearance led this reporter to ask Wayne if her leader, Joe Clark, was prepared to endorse the Focus campaign in the same way.

She admitted that she had not asked him, but said she expected Clark would be supportive. After all, she pointed out, he has a daughter who is shortly to be married, and he certainly would have wanted to protect her from child porn when she was young.

But McTeague's announcement of a round table seemed to be the impetus that would get some permanent political action on the issue.

Round tables are all the buzz these days. Occasionally, a round table is set up by an MP who wants to gather, present and test information on a particular issue, with a view to co-operative political action that bypasses the naturally adversarial nature of the House of Commons.

This round table was three hours of tough talk by several of Ontario's top police officers, investigators and prosecutors working in the child porn field. It included about sixty seconds of mind-grinding child porn photos chosen for the occasion from among 400,000 images seized from the computer-downloaded collection of a highly-educated eastern Ontario pedophile suspect.

A summary of the presentations includes the assertions that:

- *Child porn emanating from the imagination is just as harmful as that created through the use of "real children" because pedophiles use the materials to feed their urges.*
- *The advocacy of organizations like NAMBLA (North American Man-Boy Love Association) is directly damaging to children, contrary to the claims of their spokespersons.*
- *The police need legislation that will permit them to tackle this issue, because they are overloaded both by the growing activity in the computer child porn area and the complexities created by current legislative and court decisions.*

Some of the responses of the thirty-plus MPs who were at the round table, together with McTeague's skilled handling of the session, are worth noting.

The quiet presence of the NDP's Dick Proctor was telling. He is the Carleton-educated journalist-cum-politician whose note-taking skills ended Andy Scott's tenure as solicitor-general some time before. Proctor overheard Scott telling an airplane seatmate about who the government was gunning for in the APEC pepper spray scandal that was then working its way through the inquiry stage.

Liberal Dennis Mills, a strong Catholic who represents the Toronto riding of Broadview-Greenwood, a community known for its ethnic and lifestyle diversity, was strongly moved by the presenters. He urged McTeague to get the presentation in front of the national Liberal caucus, complete with the photographic images.

When it came to who should do what to get action,

there was an interesting interchange between Wayne and Tory house leader Peter MacKay.

MacKay said a supply day motion from any party, perhaps calling for the invocation of the notwithstanding clause, should be considered. Looking over to his Alliance counterparts, he told them, "You have a supply day coming up next week. I challenge you to use it."

Wayne shot eye darts at MacKay, who is young enough to be her son, and told the group that this was about protecting children, not about politics. For that reason, she said, it needed to be a government motion in order to pass the house.

She probably reined things in just in time. MPs on all sides know that they are going to have to get the support of unlikely bedfellows such as Svend Robinson and Libby Davies to effectively tackle child porn. Openly gay and lesbian politicians need the opportunity to speak out against the advocates of adult-child sex. Most heterosexual MPs, including those who are unabashedly Christian, will need to let the gays and lesbians stand with them on this particular issue.

That is why the round table has some "Sharpe" corners. And why, on this issue, it might be one of the few things that work.

While the colour and drama of adversarial and partisan political debate on the House floor captures the attention of journalists, the behind-the-scenes cross-pollination has its useful result.

John McKay is Liberal MP for Scarborough East, a founder of the Christian Legal Fellowship in Canada, member of Spring Garden Baptist Church and former chair of the National Prayer Breakfast. He suggests that much of the House debate is "pure theatre," there for effect and consumption of the people back in the riding.

He is most effective at getting Liberal and Alliance MPs singing from the same page on "social conservative" issues. He does so by not hanging out too closely with CA members in public yet working with them in developing debate strategy designed to get strong Liberal support for Alliance initiatives on both social conservative and religious liberty issues.

Is it possible to be both a Christian and a Quebec separatist? The next chapter takes a look at that question.

Chapter Three

A Sovereigntist in the Camp

On January 13, 2001, I touched on Canada's sacred solitude—the barriers created by language, culture and geography that require Christians to seem quite different in one part of the country than what their counterparts elsewhere appear to be.

For the most part, this chapter is about Daniel Turp and the way his Christian faith shapes, and is shaped by, his desire to see Quebec separate from Canada.

SACRED SOLITUDE

Recently, one Sunday morning, I had the occasion to drive to Red Deer from Calgary, where Air Canada had dumped me. In transit, I listened on the car radio to two Christian people. One was a now-deceased federalist from Alberta, the other a still-surviving but now-unseated sovereigntist from Quebec.

Ernest Manning, the twenty-five-year premier of Alberta and father to Preston, was on first. His long-running radio program, Canada's National Bible Hour, is still heard on about sixty radio stations within reach of Canadian listeners.

Manning is broadcast posthumously once a month, his content interspersed with that of other still-living preachers.

Moments later, on the CBC, was an interview with Daniel Turp, a Bloc MP from Montreal defeated in the November 27 election.

As a Manning biographer, I listened with interest to his sermon on "rightly dividing the word of truth." He was enunciating the belief held by many Christians that no godless dictator will be able to rule the world until the church of Christ is completed and removed from the earth.

In his heyday in the fifties, Manning had an audience of about 600,000 Canadians a week – more than those who tuned in to comedian Jack Benny. (Yes, I remember him. Benny was regular Sunday afternoon radio fare for me, as long as I met the mandatory parentally-shaped menu of Manning, Billy Graham and Charles E. Fuller.)

While Manning's political influence was mainly limited to Alberta, his gospel preaching gave him a national podium. Even Quebec's opposition leader, Jean Charest, from a devoutly Catholic francophone home, recalls listening every week to Manning the Baptist and cultivating a clear respect for the premier's Christian values.

Charest is now premier of Quebec, of course. And many federalists view his ascendancy as the death knell of separatism.

Charest's sometime arch-rival Preston Manning has occasionally recalled that the temper of the late 1900s would never permit a politician to publicly articulate his or her faith regularly and nationally in the way that his own father was able to do.

Daniel Turp is another story.

A nominal Catholic during his growing-up years, Turp met, fell in love with and married Barta Knoppers, daughter of a Christian Reformed minister who has served churches in both Quebec and Alberta.

Turp and Knoppers found their common church home at the Church of St. Andrew and St. Paul, a Presbyterian "cathedral" in Montreal. They grew spiritually under the open-minded and biblical preaching of James Armour, senior minister at "St. A and P" for over two decades, until recently. Turp continues to describe Armour as his spiritual mentor.

An interesting aside: Armour's son — the seventh in line to hold the "James" name — was for several years communication director in the official opposition office. The younger Armour notes that he is the first James Armour in seven generations to own property, a veiled reference to the fact that all his predecessors of the same name were Presbyterian ministers and lived in homes owned by the churches to which they ministered.

Although a lay person, the younger Armour remains a serious Christian and has a way of letting his faith shape the way he communicates within a political setting.

A few years ago I asked him how he, an urbane easterner who was part of the old-line Protestant establishment, got along communicating for the party of alleged western rednecks.

He responded, deadpan, that one thing had changed. Now, when he attended cocktail parties at which his long-time friends were present, they no longer dropped their wine glasses when they learned which political party he was working for.

One more thing about Jim Armour: he was one of two PKs (preacher's kids) in key communication roles for major Canadian political leaders. The other is Jim Munson, son of a United Church minister. He was appointed press secretary to then Prime Minister Jean Chrétien after his predecessor resigned over the flap she created by calling American President George W. Bush a "moron."

Today, Munson is a senator and Armour heads the official opposition's public affairs department.

While the passing of religious values from father to son does not always have great significance, the usefulness of having grown up in a minister's home cannot help but have an effect in aiding powerful political figures to communicate their political messages. But, back to Daniel Turp:

> *You will not move Turp from his sovereigntist position. But his Christian faith contributes to a grace and enthusiasm about the forging of a new and invigorating relationship between Quebec and Canada should there be a separation. He has as little room for the "hardliners" as the man he occasionally advises, now-departing Quebec premier Lucien Bouchard.*
>
> *A few years ago, Turp spoke to the student body of Calvin College, a Christian Reformed university in Grand Rapids, Michigan, where his brother-in-law teaches. He recounts hearing from one of his audience that his views were "truly unchristian, contrary to the teachings of Scripture and that I should be ashamed of promoting the separation of Quebec from Canada."*
>
> *Perhaps this quote from Turp, delivered at the Faith and Public Life conference held in October, 1999 at Queen's University, will, contextualized with my comments about Manning, give some meaning to the title of this piece, Sacred Solitude.*

"I am comforted at times…when in my own church, my friend Elspeth Smart smiles at me on Sundays, comes to tell me that she saw me on television and, at times, even sends me clippings of The [Montreal] Gazette, *in which her neighbour in pew 11 – myself – has made the headlines.*

"I doubt Ms. Smart, like the great many English-speaking Montrealers attending St. A and P – although they might believe that Scotland has a good case for independence – shares my view on the future of Quebec and Canada. What I do know, however, is that we share in the same faith in God."

In case Turp's long and elegant sentences obscure the import of what he is saying, permit me to translate: while the Scots advocate independence from England, those who attend St. A and P, for the most part, would not support independence of Quebec from Canada.

Interestingly, many Quebec evangelicals are separatists. They arrive at their stance, understandably, because of the way evangelicals from the rest of Canada did their work in Quebec in the early years, with the "missionary" mindset – the idea that English Canadians were bringing the gospel to an inferior, almost-foreign culture, darkened by the Union National Catholic political-religious linkages of the early and mid-twentieth century.

While francophone evangelicals accepted the evangelical gospel as freeing them from what they perceived to be the bondage of French Catholicism, they rejected the sometime rest-of-Canada assumption that French culture is inferior to the British way.

When, in April 2003, Jean Charest's Liberals replaced the Parti Québécois separatist government of Bernard Landry, a fifteen-second clip in the television coverage revealed that Daniel Turp had been elected to the Quebec National Assembly. That all happened, of course, after he had been defeated in the November 2000 federal election and returned to teaching at the University of Montreal.

My sense at the time was that his leave-taking from politics would be temporary — that he might, sometime in the future, take a run at the Parti Québécois leadership.

In May 2003, I talked about this new development in Turp's political pilgrimage.

A New Day Dawns for Daniel Turp

One of the new members of the Quebec National Assembly (read provincial legislature elsewhere in Canada) was Daniel Turp of the Parti Québécois.

Now it may be that his new MNA status will be irrelevant to the cause of Quebec nationhood because separatism is likely to be a dead issue as long as Charest is premier.

Nevertheless, Christians with political interests, both in Quebec and in other parts of Canada, will want to watch Turp with interest. He is a serious and articulate sovereigntist — in both official languages. And he is also a deeply-committed Christian. He bears watching for several reasons.

He is a constitutional lawyer who, building on his teaching role at the University of Montreal, has earned the right to a strong advisory role to a series of Parti Québécois premiers.

He served as a Bloc Québécois MP in Ottawa from 1997 to 2000, where his critiquing of the Clarity Bill helped, understandably, to win him the enmity of the Quebec federalist community. That legislation is viewed as having pretty much clipped the wings of the constitutional aspects of Quebec sovereigntist aspirations.

More Faithful than We Think

When he was defeated in the 2000 federal election, Turp went back to teaching – and to await his next political opportunity. That came with the Quebec election. And now, as one of relatively young and fresh faces in the PQ – yet possessing both focus and experience – he will likely emerge as a potential leadership successor to outgoing premier Bernard Landry.

Not to be ignored is that Turp's spouse is highly qualified in genome law and teaches in that area, also at U of M. Knoppers and Turp do not get involved in each other's professional disciplines, but their common faith provides useful mutuality.

And it is good to note the Preston Manning/Stephen Harper link in this Quebec political conundrum. Manning is often noted as being the spirit behind the Clarity Bill that so raised Turp's political ire, and Harper is known to have done much of the writing for the concept. But Turp admires Manning as both a fellow believer and a person of integrity who understands Quebec more than he might let on.

Thus, it was interesting to learn some of the background about the perspective that Manning brought to the stem cell research debate after he lost the Canadian Alliance leadership race but before he actually left the House of Commons.

Manning became the CA science and technology critic, which gave him opportunity to scrutinize the stem cell research debate that was then before the House. The pro-life view on the issue was that embryonic stem cells should not be destroyed in the interests of medical research and development.

Manning developed the arguments that were ultimately used by the CA and other pro-life people on the relevant

House committees to vouch for adult stem cell research.

And who provided the medical and legal basis for many of Manning's arguments?

Why, Barta Knoppers, of course, working out of her professional discipline and faith perspective.

Chapter Four

Faith-Based Initiatives— Pre- and Post-Bush

Two pieces I wrote in 2001 had as their focal point Marvin Olasky, who was at the time being credited for the thinking behind American President George W. Bush's "faith-based" social policy initiatives.

In the first piece, I drew a parallel between Olasky and Jake Epp, who had been health minister in Brian Mulroney's Conservative cabinet in the late eighties and early nineties.

Epp, a Mennonite Brethren from southeast Manitoba who left a high-school teaching career to go into politics in the late seventies, was the highest placed evangelical Christian in the Mulroney cabinet and the *de facto* inspiration behind what Mulroney referred to, with some affection, as his "God squad." This was a group of some thirty Tory MPs and senators who met regularly for prayer and Bible study and who tried to live out their faith in parliament.

In addition, I talked about some interesting discoveries I made about the amount of federal Human Resource Development (HRDC) funding received by Christian churches, organizations and agencies—many of whose leaders would have argued strongly for the separation of church and state. These discoveries were made while searching the big binders in the parliamentary library that listed 11,000 or so recent HRDC grants. The binders had been placed in the library during the hot-and-heavy debate over the federal government having lost track of at least a billion dollars worth of grants coming from HRDC.

THE OLASKY–EPP CONNECTION

South of the border, the new American president is creating a stir with his "compassionate conservatism." He is making it possible for faith-based domestic agencies to access federal funds to carry out social programs usually handled by government.

The concept was advanced by both Republican Bush and his Democrat opponent Al Gore, albeit more enthusiastically by Bush.

He has often advocated tapping into the immense pool of energy and motivation available in the various faith communities. His argument is that the private non-profit sector is capable of carrying out many social programs more effectively than government.

Bush's initiatives are opposed on two fronts. On one, the "separation of church and state" concept is invoked to argue that religion and the state when improperly mixed are infected with each other's faults. On the other, the voluntarism that helps make non-profit organizations tick is seen as a threat to government and organized social programmers.

In the run-up to Bush's announcement, several stories ran in both American and Canadian papers, identifying Marvin Olasky as Bush's mentor on the subject of "compassionate conservatism."

Olasky is a most influential American in making the Christian faith work in a secular world. As a distinguished journalism professor at the University of Texas, Austin, he gained prominence among Christian journalists by writing The Prodigal Press *(Westchester, IL: Crossway Books, 1988). The book proposed a vigorous Christian newspaper system to counter what he saw as the anti-Christian bias of the American news media.*

He went on to do something about it when, in the mid-nineties, he became editor-in-chief of World, *a politically conservative, theologically Calvinistic newsmagazine.*

Fast-forwarding to 2000, we find Olasky winning acceptance for his compassionate conservatism in the circles that included George W. When several of his critics suggested that he was taking the world back to the 1800s, he straightforwardly agreed. That was exactly what was needed, he maintained. Get churches, with all their real estate, moral strength and raison d'être, to do the things they increasingly gave up to government over the past 100 years.

Now, let's shift our focus to Ottawa, then back up to 1987, when Jake Epp was health minister in the Mulroney cabinet.

During his tenure, Epp introduced a proposal to provide funding for non-profit organizations that wanted to renovate or refurbish facilities for use as child-care centres. From a Christian perspective, the concept was simple. Many child-care advocates wanted a universal government-funded daycare system. Others cautioned against universality and believed such a system would work better in the for-profit corporate sector. Epp saw a third way to harness the energy of families in operating daycare centres: using the facilities of the churches to which they belonged. The upside for families and churches was that, through sharing their Christian values, they could make daycare a viable ministry and out-reach with a relevant social value.

The practical difficulty was that many churches needed renovations or additions to help them respond to this challenge. Epp's proposal was to make federal funds available, covered by covenants or agreements that would ensure that churches would continue daycare into the fore-seeable future.

That particular proposal never moved much beyond the announcement stage, but it did establish that a clearly Christian cabinet minister could, given the opportunity, propose concepts that would be win-win for both church and state.

Let's fast forward to last year's [2000] headline-grabbing debate on HRDC grants. While covering that story, I began searching through the big blue binders in the parliamentary library that listed every one of the 11,000-plus grants approved under the program. I found that hundreds of grants were given to religious organizations. Many were in the $5,000–$20,000 range and went to individual congregations across the country. Some of the largest, in the $500,000–$1 million range, were provided to such stellar Christian organizations as the Mennonite Central Committee and the Salvation Army.

There are two points to be made. One is that in Canada – in part because of the strong Catholic influence – the lines between church and state are more blurred than they are south of the border. The other is that domestic arrangements in both countries are not unlike what has gone on for decades at the international level. Non-government organizations (NGOs) receive a mix of private and government funding to carry out relief and development work that frequently ties in with the social goals of both donor and receiver nations. Some conservative Christian columnists, such as Lorne Gunter of the Edmonton Journal, *periodically question how much NGOs become beholden to the governments with which they work.*

There are trade-offs. The term "compassionate conservatism" makes that obvious. For Christian leaders, the upside of those trade-offs is that they find agreement in Jesus' counsel that we "render to Caesar the things that are Caesar's, and to God, the things that are God's" (Matthew 22:21).

A few months later, Marvin Olasky found himself in Ottawa to deliver the annual Hill Lecture, a Centre for Cultural Renewal initiative. The CCR is one of a number of think-tanks — groups who take particular public policy positions and who raise funds to research and promulgate those stances to both the public and the body politic.

The Fraser Institute, Canada West Foundation, Centre for Policy Alternatives and the McKenzie Institute all engage in think-tank work. FI focuses on a conservative approach to economic issues; CWF's area of interest is in matters that affect western Canada's political and economic interests; CFPA is a left-wing counterpart to FI; and MI studies matters relating to national security.

CCR is one group that brings a specifically religious approach to the mix, although not obviously so.

On June 30, 2001, I wrote about Olasky's visit to Ottawa. A particularly interesting part of the Hill Lecture evening was the prepared response to his talk by Claude Ryan, a devout Catholic, retired politician and newspaper publisher from Quebec.

Lloyd Mackey

DR. OLASKY COMES TO OTTAWA

(Some of the material in today's column was easier to put together because of an interview with Olasky carried out jointly by Lynne Cohen, a freelancer for Report *magazine, and me. Her electronically-transcribed tape, which she kindly e-mailed to me the next day, was particularly helpful. Thanks, Lynne.)*

Marvin Olasky teaches journalism in Texas, edits the United States' fourth largest weekly newsmagazine and, of late, is being listened to quite carefully by George W. Bush.

Last week, Olasky spent a few days in Ottawa explaining "compassionate conservatism." This is the concept on which President Bush has based his professed faith-based partnership initiatives for poverty resolution and social action.

Canada is new territory for Olasky. He admitted that social action approaches in the two nations are inherently different. The Centre for Cultural Renewal, the socio-legal think-tank under whose sponsorship he appeared, recognized that. So they had the late Claude Ryan, then éminence grise of Quebec journalism and politics, provide the response.

The difference is reflected in the constitutionally-stated goals of the two nations: Americans mandate the objectives of life, liberty and the pursuit of happiness, while Canadians go for peace, order and good government.

While accepting and, indeed, almost endorsing the biblical basis for compassionate conservatism, Ryan pointed out that its application in a Canadian setting would require adaptation to long-standing Canadian social policy. That includes recognition of Canada's relatively heavy state involvement in such things as health care, pen-

sions and what we often call the "social safety net."

Olasky acknowledged the differences. In fact, the day before, he recognized similar arguments coming from the Ottawa Citizen *editorial board. They explored with him the fact that many American poverty issues grow out of the reality that various social conditions created by slavery have never been properly resolved.*

His response was that, while Canada might not have as much of that structurally-induced poverty, he felt the main ideas behind compassionate conservatism are worth consideration in many national contexts.

The compassionate conservatism concept – and the book taking the same name – have been twenty-five years or more in the making.

Olasky was converted to Christ from Marxism in the mid-1970s, mainly through his own reading of the Bible and the influence of a Baptist minister in California. (Today, he and his wife and four children attend a conservatively-oriented Presbyterian church in Austin, Texas, where he serves as an elder.)

Much of his claim to distinction, until a few years ago, was in the teaching and practice of journalism. He has taught for the better part of two decades at the University of Texas, Austin, and, in the process, has written two books extolling the need for Christian minds and resources in the world of journalism. Much of his work in this field caused him to be dubbed the "godfather of Christian newspapering" by those of us in the field who respected, and were sometimes the subjects of, his critiques.

In the mid-nineties, Olasky became editor-in-chief of World, *a Presbyterian-rooted weekly newsmagazine that claims a circulation of about 150,000. The content and feel of the publication would find its Canadian equivalency in a mixture of* Report *and* ChristianWeek.

As this book was coming together, *Report* (known earlier in its history as *Alberta Report)* ceased publication. The Byfield family, whose vision carried the magazine for three decades, are trying to replace the magazine with a "movement" — an educational thrust that blends Christianity of an anglo-Catholic bent, social conservatism and fiscal conservatism.

About fifteen years ago, Olasky's biblical studies, screened through his remarkable move from Marxism to a conservative perspective, led him to thousands of hours of research in the Library of Congress, among other sources. He concluded that many left-filtered studies on poverty issues in the 1860–1920 period have given short shrift to the effectiveness of social action initiated by faith communities during that era.

In brief, Olasky, highpoints three consistent characteristics of compassionate conservatism that show up in both the biblical record and in the American post-civil war period: challenge, a one-on-one approach and a spiritual basis.

The challenge, he says, works when entitlements will not. A one-on-one approach replaces a misplaced trust in the efficacy of the bureaucracy. And a spiritual emphasis replaces the inclination to eliminate God from contemporary social programming.

Some of the sidelights surrounding Olasky's lecture are worth comment.

Centre for Cultural Renewal director Iain Benson had some definitional points to make, coming out of his legal background and close observation of church-state issues. He says there are several reasons to use the term "religion-based" instead of "faith-based." One of the most basic is that many people have faith but are not particularly rooted in organized or clearly-delineated religious faith.

The location of the meeting was most intriguing.

The CCR had John McKay, a Liberal MP and this year's chair of the National Prayer Breakfast, book the room. Whether it was McKay's slightly mischievous sense of humour or merely the fact that the room was the right size, we will never know. But he booked the Canadian Alliance caucus room, which has been the scene of a bit of tension lately.

That gave the attending public a chance to see who the CAers have staring down at them from the walls when they work their way through those tensions.

I won't name them all. But right in the centre are Preston Manning, Stockwell Day and Deborah Grey, with Day slightly elevated, of course. To the right is a cluster of photos including those of Manning's father, Ernest, premier of Alberta for twenty-five years in the mid-1900s, and the NDP's first leader, Tommy Douglas, a somewhat less conservative fellow Baptist. Many of the other portraits are of people of Christian conviction who helped shaped Canada's political and social spheres even before the senior Manning and Douglas were around. And they come from various points on the left-right spectrum.

After seeing the above in print, McKay contacted me to let me know, for the record, that while he would not deny the suggestion that he has a slightly mischievous sense of humour, he had no ulterior motive in booking that particular room. All the rooms available for such functions are public domains, he noted, and this happened to suit the size and nature of the crowd expected to attend the event.

The room in which Olasky, Ryan and Benson spoke created a setting that demonstrated that religious faith — in this instance, the Christian gospel — has had more to say than we might have suspected in our most pessimistic moments.

The three speakers gave hope that those past trends stand some chance of continuing.

Chapter Five

Pastors and Watchmen

The first piece in this chapter describes a group of very influential Canadian Christian leaders who work quietly in the background to bring, on a one-to-one and small-group basis, pastoral care and support to politicians of all parties.

As I explain, this was a difficult story to get at the time I wrote it, on January 8, 2002. Around Ottawa, one thing is certain: some Christians working with politicians want no publicity — even favourable — because they believe it could harm the personal relationships they develop.

Fair enough. But when the mainstream media twigs to the story, sometimes more harm develops than would have been the case if it had been written with spiritual understanding.

In this case, that did not happen. The mainstream coverage was fair, albeit brief. It offered the opportunity to put the story on the record hopefully in a way that could help some of the people who worship in the nation's largest Protestant churches to understand what their pastors are about when they quietly head off to a few days in Ottawa.

Lloyd Mackey

WHAT WERE ALL THOSE PASTORS DOING?

There they were, sitting in the House of Commons members' gallery: about a dozen pastors, each one leading one of Canada's largest evangelical churches.

And there was I, a Christian journalist, sitting in the press gallery, about fifty feet away. I was probably the only journalist present who recognized their faces. They do not appear on television regularly, like some of the politicians they had come to visit.

This scenario took place some months ago, and I found myself in conflict. As a journalist, I was observing a news story, and I was the only one who had it. As a Christian, I was sensitive to the fact that the presence of these eminent clerics could be misunderstood. Their reason for being in Ottawa could be undermined.

The ministers I saw that day are part of the Pastors' Council. The original initiative for the group came from the Christian Embassy, the Parliament Hill ministry of Campus Crusade for Christ. As it evolved and found its legs, the Council made itself informally accountable to the Evangelical Fellowship of Canada. In turn, the EFC is a broad enough body to draw feedback and counsel from over thirty different denominations as well as several hundred evangelical churches whose own affiliations link them to mainline denominations.

The makeup of the particular group I heard that day included the pastors of large churches in cities across Canada from such denominations as Anglican, Alliance, Evangelical Missionary, Presbyterian, Pentecostal, Baptist and Mennonite. The churches represented have weekend attendances ranging from 1,000 to 4,000, for a total of about

120,000. The council's then chair was Vern Heidebrecht, senior minister at Northview Community Church in Abbotsford, a Mennonite Brethren congregation whose attendance would be in the upper end of that range.

Heidebrecht is careful to note that the Council is not an advocacy group or a lobbying organization. Its agenda is simple: to meet with, pray with, listen to and dialogue with politicians of any party open to the idea. Among them, the various pastors are able to open doors to MPs' offices in all parties. Cabinet ministers and key opposition critics are among those who appreciate their occasional visits to Ottawa.

One of the reasons for that broad acceptance, Heidebrecht suggests, is that the pastors are not Ottawa-based but are part of community life in cities scattered across Canada. They are meeting with, preaching to and working among thousands of people who, in turn, are active in their own communities.

Those people come from across the spectrum, as attendees at any megachurch will readily note. Politically, professionally and in terms of family status, they are an eclectic bunch. Their commonality is that the leadership they get from their pastors is rooted in the centrality of the Bible, Christ and the new birth as the Christian reason to be. Their social action, evangelism, teaching and fellowship grow out of those basics.

That means such churches, for the most part, do not endorse political parties, candidates or individual politicians, even when those people are members of their churches. And they will tend to caution against using church directories for political recruiting purposes, especially if it appears that such activity could be seen as intimidating.

Yet, the pastors also encourage their congregations to be politically informed and active. They know that, even in an alien and often adversarial society, the opportunities for Christian lifestyle, action and witness are plentiful and fulfilling.

From time to time, I will enjoy talking about the Council. I will remain conflicted. The story needs to be told, but in such a way as to let the group do its gospel work across the political spectrum.

One day, not long after doing the above piece, I received a call from one of the people responsible for communication in Watchmen for the Nations, the organization highlighted in the next article, which was written on May 27, 2002. The caller wanted to know how Watchmen could link up with the Pastors' Council. I said that I had to make contact, and left it there.

Watchmen, as readers will note, represents a subset of evangelical Christianity that is both charismatic and prophetic in approach. It is a different way of "doing politics Christianly," and some of its leaders sometimes communicate the impression that they believe it is the only way because it is actually working to bring in the kingdom.

I believe it is important for the broader church to understand what people such as those involved with Watchmen for the Nations are doing. Thus, the next piece hopefully provides some food for thought.

KEEPING WATCH

A look at the Web site www.watchmen.org is always interesting, often inspiring and, at times, surprising. It is the site of a ministry known as Watchmen for the Nations, founded by the respected Robert Birch, a Vancouver charismatic Christian leader now well into his nineties.

A few years ago, Pastor Birch handed the mantle over to David Demian, a Vancouver surgeon who has emerged as the movement's key prophetic spokesperson, and to Demian's wife, Ruth.

Watchmen is probably best known in the broader Christian community for instigating periodic events, each of which is known as The Gathering of the Nations or the Gathering for short. Such events usually draw several thousand people each and have been held in Whistler, Victoria and Winnipeg.

The Gatherings are deep, worshipful, high-energy events. I attended one in Victoria in 1996, where about 4,000 gathered in the Memorial Arena. The major features were:

- *Some biblically-based teaching sessions featuring high-profile figures such as David Mainse, David Demian and Denys Blackmore of Every Home for Christ*
- *Lots of contemporary Christian music, some influenced by the Vineyard movement*
- *A two-hour session of high energy dancing and jumping, generally known in the charismatic movement as "dancing in the Spirit"*

Two years ago in Ottawa, Watchmen sponsored an event during which several dozen Canadian Christian leaders met with survivors of the St. Louis, a World War II ship of Jewish refugees that was refused permission to drop its human cargo in Canada. Among the apologies proffered during the meeting was one on behalf of a deputy immigration minister who was a strong and respected Christian leader, but who also apparently harboured some anti-Semitic views. It was that man who apparently gave the order to turn the ship away. The apology came from the man's nephew, now a clergyman in southwestern Ontario.

A common characteristic of the Gatherings, including the St. Louis event, is that, inevitably, a reconciliation initiative develops. In Whistler, it was between aboriginals and Caucasians; in Victoria, between generations.

Watchmen's Web site says the movement is a "prophetic prayer team called together by the leading of the Holy Spirit to serve the Body of Christ. We seek to hear what the Holy Spirit is saying to the churches in this hour and to obey the Lord by voicing what He gives from His Heart."

The group's leaders (known in Watchmen parlance as "Fathers and Mothers") are household names in the charismatic movement, some of whose influence extends respectively into other parts of the Christian spectrum. They are:

- Bob and Margaret Birch (the founders of Watchmen)
- John and Lorrie White (John, now deceased, was a psychiatrist-author and Vineyard pastor)
- George and Joyce Johnson (George is a well-regarded mainstream Pentecostal clergyman)
- Jim and Marie Watt (Jim is a Messianic pastor)
- Alistair and Marie Petrie (Alistair is an Anglican minister very involved in the encouragement of the Transformation videos)
- Gordon and Nancy Patterson (Gordon is a Baptist minister in Victoria; he and Alistair are arguably the most mainstream Protestants of the group)
- Peter and Donna Jordan (I am not acquainted with this couple so can share no further information)
- Gideon and May Chiu (Gideon is pastor of

Vancouver's Church of Zion, an international charismatic church)

- *Danny and Lu Cheung (they are associated in ministry with the Chius)*
- *David and Ruth Demian*

The Gatherings are touted as having no other agenda but that of the Holy Spirit. However, they are obviously shaped by the prophecies their leaders believe God has given to them. One such, which Demian has posted on the Web site, states: "We [Canada] are being asked to walk closely with the leadership of Taiwan and Switzerland and the city of Hong Kong, imparting to them the principles that we have learned from our journey in Canada. We will help them identify and connect their national Fathers and Mothers who, in turn, can begin to seek the Lord for their own destiny."

This brings us to the point of today's piece.

Last September, a leadership Gathering (by invitation only) took place in Kelowna. Its proceedings are reported on the Web site, including a presentation from Stockwell Day, then leader of the opposition.

Some of the phraseology with respect to Jesus' sacrifice and the need for good men to act to combat evil became regular items in the presentations Day made to church groups during his second leadership campaign. People will interpret those statements differently, depending on their political or spiritual perspectives.

Keeping in mind the prophecy that is causing Demian to keep some of Watchmen's focus on Taiwan, let's continue the story.

Two weeks ago [May 2002], Day, now newly-minted as Canadian Alliance foreign affairs critic, went to Taiwan with his wife, Valorie, and several MPs who supported him in his second leadership bid, along with their spouses. All of them are serious Christian believers, apparently open to Watchmen's prophetic approach.

They were invited to Taiwan to attend the country's National Prayer Breakfast. As far as I can gather, the breakfast was not a Watchmen event but was one tied in with the groups that put on the National Prayer Breakfast in Ottawa, the Presidential Prayer Breakfast in Washington and similar events in 160 other countries. Watchmen spokesperson Peg Byars confirms that Watchmen facilitated getting Day to Taiwan, but indicated that the bill was paid by some sector of the Taiwanese government, not by any religious organizations.

It is good that Day appears to be seeking the counsel of the people at Watchmen as he carries out his foreign affairs critic role. Evangelical Christians of all stripes – not just charismatics and fundamentalists – have worthwhile counsel to offer anyone charged with the responsibility of understanding the workings of the nations. We are, after all, internationalists whose educational, mission and development activity gives us good reason to bring useful perspectives to bear on foreign affairs. That there are biblical undercurrents to what we see and hear is an important adjunct.

There is a biblical proverb that might help people like Day, his government counterpart, Bill Graham, and anyone else in the House involved in foreign affairs issues. In the King James Version, the proverb elegantly suggests that "in the multitude of counsellors there is safety."

Somewhere among that multitude there will be a prophet or two – or at least a second or third sound opinion.

A Gathering was also scheduled to take place in Charlottetown. That happened in August 2002.

Stockwell and Valorie Day were there, and they were prayed over and "released" for unspecified spiritual leadership by the Fathers and Mothers, in a Sunday morning worship session.

What happened there, and what has happened since, is a very sensitive subject, open to tension between people who believe that Stockwell Day is definitely God's man for Canada and those who believe he might or might not be. Some of the people who are working for him behind the scenes, both in Watchmen and in other Christian ministries, continue to watch for failings in the current political leadership in Canada. They watch for ruptures that might return him to the leadership of a political party and a shot at the prime ministership.

The difficulty with such an approach is that it leads to political behaviour — not on Day's part but among some of his supporters — that can be construed as spiritual one-upmanship and the playing of the persecution card.

One of David Demian's prophecies, issued in the late spring of 2003, was that the year 2003 would be a year of division among Christian people, between those who sought intimacy with Christ and those who wanted to go about God's work the same old way.

When Christians across Canada read this book, there will be an opportunity to observe whether this was a self-fulfilling prophecy or whether it really represented a more spiritual way of doing faith and politics.

Day should, as the foreign affairs critic for the official opposition, continue to get his counsel from Christians of all stripes, not just from those who make the point that they are speaking prophetically. He will do well to function as do John Manley and Preston Manning —

being as shrewd as snakes and as innocent as doves. And he can learn much from that nineteenth-century evangelical reformer William Wilberforce.

Chapter Six

Bobbie: Getting It Together

The featured piece in this chapter is a good one to follow our consideration of the Pastors' Council and Watchmen for the Nations. The article has provided the most appreciative feedback of almost anything I have written. It came out of my visit to the Presidential Prayer Breakfast in Washington, in February 2002, and was written a couple of weeks later.

Because many of the events in connection with that breakfast are off the record, I made the decision that, although this story needed to be told, I could not identify the specific member of Congress who is the subject. Perhaps there will be an occasion to do so one day.

Also, although this is an American story, it is one that can prove helpful to people wanting to understand the Protestant/Catholic dichotomy that makes up Christian influence on the body politic in Canada. Indeed, there are about twice as many Catholics per capita in Canada and half as many Protestants than in the United States. So the "Bobbie" story has even more relevance here than it would south of the border.

Lloyd Mackey

BOBBIE GOT SAVED TONIGHT

Bobbie was a thirteen-year-old boy living in a mid-western American town. He grew up to be a member of the United States House of Representatives.

In that capacity, he told the following story at one of the Presidential Prayer Breakfast events I attended earlier this month [February 2002] in Washington. I have shortened it and kept the identities vague enough to honour the off-the-record nature of these events.

Bobbie lived on the same street as six other thirteen-year-old neighbour boys. They were all part of St. Joseph's Catholic Church where Father McGonigal was the priest.

That spring, one of the boys moved away. Another thirteen-year-old boy moved into the same house. His name was Greg, and he was, of all things, a Baptist.

Bobbie's mother cautioned him. This new boy, she said, might be very nice, but be careful. Baptists recruit, and they especially like to recruit Catholics.

All went well for about six months.

Then, one afternoon, Greg asked his six new friends if they would come with him to Pisgah Heights Baptist Church the next Wednesday evening. He would get a prize if he could bring more visitors than anyone else.

Their parents gave the boys permission to go with Greg – with the caution not to get recruited.

Off they went, in Greg's mom's station wagon. Up the stairs they ran, into Pisgah Heights Baptist Church. First stop was for punch and cookies. The boys found the Baptists to be very nice, and they enjoyed the pleasant and slightly sanctified banter of the various people they met.

Then, into the sanctuary they trooped for the Baptist

Family Night meeting. Greg sat them right in the front row. He was so proud his buttons almost burst, and he won the prize for bringing the most visitors.

The pastor had an interesting message. He ended it in good Baptist style, with an invitation for those who wanted to take a stand for Christ to come forward to the front of the church.

The Baptists sat on their hands. Nobody moved. The pastor repeated the invitation and, still, there was nary a stir.

Bobbie felt badly for the pastor. He remembered that, just last week, Father McGonigal had told him in confirmation class that he should always, whenever the opportunity presented itself, take a stand for Christ.

So Bobbie went forward and stood with the pastor. And he was glad he did.

As Greg's mom drove the boys home in her station wagon, Greg told her that "Bobbie got saved tonight."

When Bobbie got home, he told his mom, "Greg says I got saved tonight."

Bobbie's mom was livid.

"I told you they would try to recruit you," she said, marching him out the front door and down the street to the house where Father McGonigal lived, next door to St. Joseph's.

When the priest answered the door, Bobbie's mom told him the Pisgah Heights story, ending it with the urgent request that he "turn Bobbie back into a Catholic."

Father McGonigal paused a moment, then advised Bobbie's mom that he had told the boys in confirmation class a few days before that good Catholics should be willing to take a stand for Christ any time, any place.

"Bobbie did what any good Catholic should. He will be

okay. Besides, it is 9:30. Go on home. It is time we all got some sleep."

Today, three decades later, Bobbie is Bob, and he is still a Catholic. He loves his wife and three kids. And he meets every week with six other members of Congress. They gather to:
- *Get to know Christ better*
- *See what the Bible says about how they should live*
- *Make sure they walk straight*
- *Be accountable to each other and to God*
- *Pray together*

His buddies are all Christians of several different stripes — and at several points along their faith pilgrimages. Politically, some are conservative Republicans; others are liberal Democrats. But their common faith in Christ helps them to do politics Christianly.

One other item coming out of that Washington prayer breakfast was the witness of the leader of one unidentified Middle East nation, who told the crowd that "I am a Muslim who has put Jesus in my heart."

It is a statement with a king-sized conundrum attached to it.

But across the body of Christ, in post-9/11 international relations and domestic politics, I see the simultaneous efforts of disparate groups of people to reach out and improve relations with Jewish and Muslim people. In some ways these efforts seem to be rooted in self-survival or, at the very least, survival of the Christian community.

On one hand, we find groups who have decided that it is no longer necessary to try to win Jewish people to Christ. Such groups espouse what is sometimes called "two covenant theology." They teach that God has a different covenant with Israel and with Jewish people than he does with Christians. In effect, they believe that when the Messiah comes, both Jews and Christians will recognize him. Some such teachers suggest the prophecies of Psalm 22:27, where it says: "All the ends of the earth will remember and turn to the Lord and all the families of the nations will bow down before him, for dominion belongs to the Lord and he rules over the nations."

The American television newsmagazine *60 Minutes* has provided some coverage of this kind of thinking, which is currently espoused by people such as Texas tele-vangelist John Hagee and, in Canada, by those at Canada Christian College (CCC) and Watchmen for the Nations.

A few months ago, I asked CCC president Charles McVety about the "two covenant theology," when he spoke on Parliament Hill in the interests of encouraging Christians to combat anti-Semitism. He strongly denied that this was a "forked tongue" kind of theology in which Christians were asked to support Israel recognizing that, when Messiah comes, there would be spiritual genocide of the Jewish people.

He bluntly stated only that Jews and Christians alike will recognize the Messiah, so it is, in effect, a win-win situation.

On the other hand, many Christians reach out to Muslims in the same way. Among them: the Robert Schuller/Crystal Cathedral organization and some of its spinoffs, who help churches located in high immigration areas to understand their Muslim neighbours.

I saw that kind of program operating six years ago — before 9/11 — at Bromley Road Baptist Church, located on Ottawa's west side in a community that has become over fifty percent Muslim in recent years. For several weekly sessions, church members and Muslim neighbours gathered about 100-strong in the church gym to explore together their similarities and differences. One session was devoted to sharing what the Qur'an and the Muslim religion teach about Jesus.

Muslim leaders who abhor the radical "terror in the name of God" mindset linked with their religion want to make sure that Christians understand they are on side with them.

Each Saturday in the *Ottawa Citizen*, four clerics of different religions answer a question of current interest. On July 26, 2003, the question was: "*Time Magazine* recently ran an article about American evangelicals' plans to target Muslim countries with the intent of saving them from hell by converting their citizens. How does your religious group approach conversion?"

The answer from Abdul Rashid, an Ottawa Muslim leader and a member of the Christian–Muslim Dialogue, noted, particularly with respect to Islamic belief about Jesus, that: "[Evangelicals] may be surprised to learn that acceptance of Jesus Christ, peace be upon him, is an essential part of Muslim creed. Muslims believe that the message of Jesus Christ, 'So fear Allah and obey me. It is Allah who is my Lord and your Lord; then worship Him. This is a way that is straight' (3:50,51) was in unison with the message of all the prophets of God, including Noah, Abraham, Moses and Muhammad, peace be upon them all. The Holy Qur'an contains the most beautiful and heart-warming descriptions of Jesus, his birth, his miracles and his message (19:16–41)."

That kind of religious diplomacy gives some context to the Muslim political leader who says he has Jesus in his heart.

The seeming lowering of the Christian–Jewish theological barriers helps one understand the lay leader in a synagogue in one large Canadian city who attends a weekly Bible study in a downtown tower in order to nurture his personal commitment to Jesus, the Christ.

I can understand that if either of the men referred to were to leave the religion that is an integral part of their culture to join a Christian church, they would be making a decision with grave consequences.

Yet, if what they are doing lines up with the evangelical emphasis that becoming a Christian involves inviting Jesus into your heart and life and asking him to help you live like he did, then what are you? Christian, Jew, Muslim — or something in between?

What can be said with some certainty is that when people do politics Christianly, they find ways of reconciling and building bridges. And when evangelical Christians are doing it, they do it in the name of Jesus.

The next piece was written October 6, 2001, just a few weeks after 9/11. It focuses on a short interview I had with Rahim Jaffer, a young Canadian Alliance MP and the only Muslim in the House of Commons.

THE MUSLIM MYSTIQUE

Two things I have learned to know much better since September 11: the words of the American national anthem and the various parts of the Qur'an that speak of war and peace. Not that I have come to the end of learning in those areas, but I have certainly been exposed to repetition, conjecture, punditry, earnest entreaties and offhand throwaway lines.

Today, we will leave the anthem aside and try to reflect for a few moments on the Muslim mystique. The best way I know how, as a Christian journalist whose theology is not very systematic, is to make some comparisons and contrasts between some of the things I have been learning about Islam and the Christian world and culture I know best.

Two weeks ago, I referred in passing to Rahim Jaffer (CA, Edmonton-Strathcona), the only Muslim member of Parliament. As far as I can tell, I was the first journalist in this particular round to ask him what kind of Muslim he is. The reply: Ismaili.

My response was: "Isn't that the kind run by the Aga Khan?"

Right.

It has been reinforced during the past few weeks that there are two major Islamic divisions, Shia and Sunni, as well as a pretty substantial number of Ismailis.

If we were to overlay a Christian denominational spectrum on its Muslim equivalent, we might well find — at the risk of oversimplification — the following: the Ismailis would be like Anglicans, the Sunnis would line up with the Catholics or the United Church, and the Shi'ites might emerge more like Southern Baptists or Pentecostals.

And where would Osama bin Laden fit?

Likely pretty much off the spectrum, out there where we find white supremacist churches, Jim Jones, the Branch Davidian and Timothy McVeigh. They all were or are quite capable of quoting the Bible to maintain their position, just as bin Laden's speeches and activities seem to draw on counsel from the Qur'an.

At best, people in mainstream Christianity would refer to those above-mentioned groups as "Christian deviations" or, more likely, as "cults." Or they would try to be clear that such groups really have nothing to do with either the Bible or the Christ of the Christian gospel.

Some of these thoughts came to me after one reader gently told me, "Your next-door neighbour who is a Muslim is quite different from a Muslim-dominated society."

We hear much, for example, about the Sudan, where a militant Islamic government stands accused of engaging in genocide against Christians and animists in the southern part of the nation. That particular example has been a rallying cry for a whole range of Christian groups across the theological spectrum to press for a Canadian oil company to get out of Sudan. Only in that way, the Christian groups insist, will Canadian complicity in that genocide be neutered.

In Afghanistan, pre-September 11, the plight of eight Christian aid workers who were charged with trying to convert Muslims to Christianity was becoming a major international story. And now, the workers are being used as bargaining chips as the Afghans try to ward off major military attacks on their soil.

There is a stark contrast between the bearded, turbaned Taliban clerics who run Afghanistan and the debonair, open-faced Rahim Jaffer. That is why I asked him a second question in preparation for my "doing politics christianly..." column two weeks ago [September 2001]. "Do Christians ever try to proselytize you?" I queried, knowing that close to a third of MPs in his party claim to adhere to the particular kind of Christianity that places strong emphasis on evangelism and conversion. These kinds of Christians are especially intent on reaching "unreached" people groups – which have evidently dropped from over 20,000 down to about 12,000 in the last two decades since missiologist Ralph Winter started cataloguing them.

An unreached people group, by generally accepted missiological definitions, is one that has no significant Christian church presence. So there are both individual and cultural ramifications. If you have no churches in a group, you seek out converts; then you organize them into congregations and denominations. These new Christian presences become competition for the dominant or established religions.

All this church planting gets pretty professional and sophisticated. It plants the seeds for community and social transformation – and perhaps for ferment and persecution.

Jaffer obviously did not know he was supposed to be a conversion target. He said the Christians he knew – both his parliamentary colleagues and the young women, some of them avowed Christians, with whom he socializes – were very interested in his faith, especially since September 11. Not that he was trying to convert them, either. But he is a part of North America's fastest growing religion.

Returning to where we started: I hope that this comparison and contrast exercise will be helpful in identifying some of the dynamics that exist cross-culturally, cross-politically and cross-nationally.

If there is anything that will grow out of September 11 for Christians who are involved politically, it is that our communication with the rest of the world will be more strategic and more pointed than ever. The idea of being as shrewd as snakes and as harmless as doves – and not the other way around – will become increasingly important. And so will good listening.

Chapter Seven

The National Magnet

My sojourn in Ottawa began in the run-up to the Billy Graham National Capital Region mission, in June 1998.

In many places in North America, Christian community newspapers — transdenominational publications distributed mainly in churches to the "average person in the pew" — have been jump-started by a Billy Graham mission. Such was the case in Ottawa. In the wake of many people coming to new spiritual life through the influence of the mission comes a new interest in becoming a part of the Christian community. With that interest comes a willingness to get involved in Christian stewardship, service, fellowship and education. A newspaper working in co-operation with the churches in a community helps to network in a way that facilitates all those neat things happening.

A nation's capital becomes a special magnet for those who seek spiritual renewal in their lives and communities. In the wake of the Billy Graham mission, there were many new groups formed whose leaders believed they had a special God-given task in the interests of encouraging spiritual renewal and healing.

Lloyd Mackey

As an Ottawa-focused Christian journalist, I heard frequently from people who were drawn to the capital in order to begin a new ministry or enhance something already in existence.

Three types of activity were evident:

- In existing churches, pastors and other leaders were motivated and equipped to help integrate new Christians who had come into their fellowship as a result of the Billy Graham visit. Among such churches were Metropolitan Bible, Woodvale Pentecostal, Kanata Baptist, Kanata Wesleyan, St. Paul's Presbyterian, All Saints Lutheran, Life Centre, St. Mary's Roman Catholic, Dominion-Chalmers United, City Church...and many more. There were many smaller churches, too, that experienced post-Graham reinvigoration. In the cases of those churches, the thrust was often on making them more energized in communicating with their own neighbourhood.
- There were many new "church plants." Some came from the traditional evangelical streams. One such was Sequoia Community Church, which received considerable backing from the Southern Baptists—coincidentally, the denomination that ordained Billy Graham. Others came from the more charismatic streams, and their leaders unabashedly spoke of having received prophecies from the Lord that a great revival would sweep Canada and that it would begin in Ottawa. Harvest Glory was one of these, a branch of an American group led by the late Ruth Ward Hefflin. She had popularized the concept that one of the signs of God's visitation on a church was the falling of gold dust on its people or the mystical

92

planting of a gold filling into a worshipper's tooth.

- There was the focus on the Hill and the Peace Tower itself. That place had always been a point of gathering and inspiration for Christians of all stripes. One of the smaller but nonetheless inspirational gatherings has been the Easter Sunrise Service, just beneath the Peace Tower, sponsored annually by the Ottawa Evangelical Ministerium. David Mainse of "100 Huntley Street" periodically arranged a July 1 gathering to encourage Christians to be patriotic Canadians. The Cry, a youth-oriented gathering, drew about 7,000 young people from across Canada in the summer heat of 2002. Their message was that the Christian youth of Canada was crying out for that sweeping national revival.

Never far from the surface in these three kinds of manifestations, particularly those in the last category, was the reminder of one of the biblical texts carved into the stonework on the Peace Tower. The text is: "He shall have dominion from sea to sea" (Psalm 72:8).

The fact that at one time Canada was known—and is still legally designated—as the Dominion of Canada has given great inspiration to many Canadian Christians over the years. So the "dominion" text becomes very special, although the interpretation and application differs depending on the mindset of the particular Christian leader.

Also, the fact that the text continues in Holy Writ from that phrase on the Peace Tower to say "and from the river to the ends of the earth" is an opportunity for some leaders to apply it directly to contemporary Canada. After all, what other nation has the mighty St. Lawrence River and the Great Lake System it drains at its southernmost extremity and the North Pole at the other end?

To some of the people who orate at the Peace Tower, the "dominion" inspiration is pretty literal. They believe that Christ will indeed set up his kingdom in Canada, and that it will happen when the nation's leaders recognize the dominion of God. Often, they have in mind a particular person who could become that leader, the one who can properly represent God in a national structure that comes very close to the description of a "theocracy" — as contrasted with "democracy." They are careful not to suggest that elections would cease to be or that the government will be led by clerics in some Christian reflection of an Islamic republic. To say that a majority of Christians hold to that particular view would be a serious skewing of the facts.

Earlier, I referred to the three different approaches flowing out of the spiritual atmosphere created in the wake of the 1998 Billy Graham mission. In describing the most doctrinaire form of "dominion" inspiration, I would be careful to point out that most Ottawa Christians probably treat the dominion passage more as a spiritual influence. They would suggest that Christ established his dominion in the hearts of his people and they, in turn, spread his influence and renewal through the service they do, the relationships they build and the lives they live in the name of Christ.

Much goes on in those existing churches that I mentioned to keep the special status of their city as the national capital in front of the regular worshippers. Not many MPs regularly attend an Ottawa church, because most of them are in their own ridings on the weekend. But those who do form a link with a capital-based congregation find themselves willingly, for the most part, under pastoral care.

It is a matter of public record that both Jean Chrétien and Paul Martin regularly attend Catholic mass and take their faith pretty seriously, although neither buys into the idea that all their personal beliefs can or should be translated into public policy. During his tenure, Chrétien always listened carefully to Ottawa Archbishop Marcel Gervais, both publicly and, at times, privately. But he did not always ask "How high?" when the good bishop said "Jump!"

John Manley, who grew up in Metropolitan Bible Church and learned a lot about leadership in that church's Christian Service Brigade, traces his conversion to serious faith to making Cursillo in an Anglican setting. He and his wife, Judith, are part of a Presbyterian church in his riding and he has been a frequent speaker on the prayer breakfast circuit. As indicated elsewhere in this volume, his political "mentor" is the nineteenth-century evangelical reformer, William Wilberforce.

Canadian Alliance leader Stephen Harper attends an Ottawa-area Christian and Missionary Alliance church when he is in Stornoway, the official opposition residence in Ottawa. In addition to regular attendance, however, he keeps in touch with his pastor, looking to him as sort of an informal Protestant equivalent to the widely-practised Catholic concept of having a spiritual director. Harper was once heard to comment (somewhat tongue-in-cheek we are sure), when it was suggested that he attend a Presbyterian church when he settled in Ottawa, that he wanted "something more conservative than that!"

While Christian cabinet ministers and MPs from the Ottawa area find an Ottawa church home, those from most of the rest of Canada will seek spiritual fellowship and direction in their home cities. The influence of Ottawa churches remains potentially strong in the lives of the Christian bureaucrats. Hundreds of them, perhaps even a few thousand, are scattered most Sundays into Protestant and Catholic, English and French churches in and around the capital.

It is for this reason that I suggest the "invisible dominion" might be far stronger than even the most optimistic theocrat believes. The politicians and bureaucrats are surrounded — even swamped with — pastors, spiritual directors, Christian advocates, prophets and more.

However, to come to the core of this chapter, I want to talk about the prophets and the prophetic as they relate to the Ottawa body politic. To introduce some points on the matter, I have chosen a piece from "doing politics christianly…" written on March 10, 2001. Then, I will wrap with "do" and "don't" lists about how to handle prophets and what they say around the capital.

THE THREE FACES OF A PROPHET

"Some Christians deserve to be persecuted."

I could hardly believe my ears. The week before hearing those words, I had been reporting that several Christians were involved in a campaign to reduce the debt of the poorest countries while others worked to reduce religious persecution.

Advocates in both camps argued that they were fighting death. Children die for lack of medical and social services in countries where the cost of debt rules out provision of those services and religious persecution often results in the death of innocent children who are part of a persecuted group.

The comment about persecution-deserving Christians

came at a moment of unintended candour from someone who objected to my seeming to give equal weight to both issues.

Many Christians advocate for the issue of debt forgiveness for poor nations. Many, by so doing, see themselves as involved in a prophetic ministry. They suggest that numerous declarations of Old Testament writers speak timelessly to issues of economic and social justice.

That is one of the faces of a prophet.

I write about it this week because I am discovering that there is no shortage of prophets in and around Parliament Hill. To understand the work they do, I find it helpful to categorize the prophets.

For our purposes today, there are three faces. They come out of three different Christian traditions: liberal, dispensational and charismatic. From where I sit, some in each camp find it difficult to respect – or even understand – the prophetic utterances of those in the other folds.

The *liberal* tradition is represented by the example I used above, as well as by the previous story about Robert Smith, the former United Church moderator. I will have more to say in the next chapter about this as I trace the Christian advocacy spectrum from left to right. The point of this particular exploration is to understand how people from different parts of the Christian spectrum each utilize prophecy and the prophetic Scriptures in different – and in variously conflicting or complementary – ways.

Social liberals who are involved in Christian advocacy work draw from the Old Testament prophecies, especially Isaiah and Jeremiah, that will help them to be able to advocate for public policy rooted in liberal or left-leaning traditions.

Lloyd Mackey

*The millennium books, movies and videos such as the
Left Behind series are the contemporary versions of the **dis-
pensational** teachings that developed in the early and
middle twentieth century. Among the key teachers were C.I.
Scofield of the Scofield Bible, Charles E. Fuller of the "Old
Fashioned Revival Hour," H.A. Ironside of Chicago's Moody
Memorial Church — and long-time Alberta premier Ernest
Manning, father of Preston.*

*These teachers all advocated reading the Bible alongside
the newspaper, because they believed many of the Bible's
prophetic passages found fulfilment in the unfolding of those
news stories.*

*In twenty-first-century terms, the dispensational
prophetic school urges politicians to use the Bible as one means
to interpret current events in such far-flung places as Russia
and Israel. Cataclysmic events such as the recent earthquakes
[2001] are used, sometimes more subtly than others, to draw
attention to God's all-seeing eye and outstretched arm.*

*The **charismatic** face grows out of the approach that
says God gives chosen people the ability to speak a word of
prophecy or use a public occasion to frame a prophetic message. Erika Kubassek, one prime example, arrived on the Hill
on the day former US president Bill Clinton was in Ottawa
in the late 90s. She picked up temporary press credentials,
went to Clinton's press conference and asked if he saw recent
natural disasters as messages from above about society's
moral decay and penchant for abortion. Clinton replied that
"the real moral message here is that as we all get richer and
use more of the resources God has given us, we are being
called upon to take greater care of them."*

*Some of the prophets are loners who seem to act, at
times, on impulse. They maintain that those impulses are*

God-directed and they have little difficulty identifying their work as prophetic.

Others are parts of groups who research, strategize and speak after careful collaboration. They prepare briefs, bring specialists on certain issues to the Hill to meet politicians, appear before committees and make statements to the media after major Supreme Court decisions. They leave it to others to decide if what they are doing is prophetic.

Prophets are human beings with mixed motives, like the rest of us. Some have fair-sized egos and enjoy the attention they get — even when it seems they are being put down by their opponents. Some speak out of well-developed philosophies or ideologies. They know their subject and speak with certainty.

Some know, absolutely, that they are right and their opponents wrong.

Some seem more intent on attacking certain politicians whom they oppose than on trying to create some understanding for their own particular message. They would, like Jonah, be disappointed if the target of their prophecies actually repented and did what they wanted.

Whether they are loners or parts of organized Christian groups or ministries, prophets have an important role to play on the Hill. Good politicians know that they should treat them well because they never know when their message might, indeed, be from God. Or, like Clinton, they might be adept enough to try speaking prophetically themselves.

I wanted to include this analysis of the "prophetic" on Parliament Hill, particularly drawing on my reference to the fact that the prophets, by the very nature of the certainty and, often, dogmatism they bring to their work, do not help the Christian community to speak with one voice.

As it happens, I grew up in and received the theological part of my education within a tradition that was rooted in dispensationalism. There was a little ditty students liked to sing in the hallways of the kinds of schools represented by the one at which I studied in the late fifties and early sixties. A takeoff on the old gospel hymn "My Hope is Built on Nothing Less than Jesus' Blood and Righteousness," the ditty quipped, "My hope is built on nothing less than Scofield notes and Scripture Press."

That was one part of my early Christian pilgrimage. The second was an understanding of the church that recognized pastors, evangelists and teachers as important to the continuing task of communicating the gospel.

The other two designations (apostles and prophets) were considered, in the dispensationalist scheme of things, to have completed their work in Christianity's first century. The people who taught me the Christian faith maintained that all the prophecy anyone needs is couched in the Scriptures of the Old and New Testament—and no one should add to or take away from that record.

So my background tends to inform about prophets in a way that says, in the first instance: "Okay. You may be right when you say you are a prophet or when you say God has told you to tell the politicians something. Or, you might be wrong. And I, as a Christian, have the right to either accept or reject your validity. You should not penalize, berate or hex me because I choose not to accept, without reservation, what you have to say."

As a Christian journalist, I find it helpful, in the longer term, to be skeptical but not necessarily cynical about the claims of the prophets. Skepticism means that I try to go below the surface of what the prophet is saying. Cynicism implies a touch of bitterness or disdain for the prophet, which is not conducive to good communication. The skeptic listens with goodwill if not with unquestioning acceptance. The cynic questions motives and attributes less-than-savoury purposes to the activities of the prophet.

As the years have passed, I have informally codified "do" and "don't" lists to help me keep in check, as a Christian journalist, in covering what the prophets have to say.

Do...

- Listen carefully to what the prophet has to say. Many prophets, even if they preface what they have to say with the affirmation that God has given them the word on it, have studied the issue and are well informed about it.
- Find out who is behind the prophet. Is he or she a loner, or are there people of credibility backing the statements being made? And are they people who will bring independent thinking to the prophet's proclamations, or are they merely rubber stamps or "yes" people?
- Ask penetrating questions. Especially ask questions about the biblical basis for the point being made. Some of the more flamboyant prophets have little biblical basis for what they say. Yet, there are those who try to bring forward a current application from the great themes and issues explored by the biblical prophets for the leaders of their day. They speak out of a well-formulated biblical background but do not include the results of their biblical exegesis in the briefs they present to the politicians. There is a good reason for this.

Most politicians would develop glassy-eyed stares within the first few minutes. Even those who are devout Christians might be good for a twenty-minute sermon or a half-hour Bible study once every week or two. The volume of paper and the verbosity with which most politicians have to deal is overwhelming. But asking biblically literate questions should well ferret out the basis for the brief, if there is one.

- Reinterpret the person who says he or she is pro-claiming "The Truth." In any one month, I will listen to several people who claim to have a corner on "The Truth." One of the first actions of a listener with healthy skepticism will be to check "The Truth" against the facts. Without a factual basis, truth will not fly. Often, an implied arrogance in the "Truthteller's" presentation gets in the way of the message. Sometimes, the reinterpretation is in the form of expressing a prophet's declaration as his or her deeply-held values. The proclaimer of "The Truth" might see that as a cop-out, an act of cowardice, but, in fact, it could turn out to be a humble and faithful rep-resentation of what he or she is saying. Stripped of its arrogance, it finds immeasurably better acceptance with those who must consider it for inclusion in any public policy consideration.

- Follow the money trail. Even prophets have to eat. And some find they can make a very good living from what they do. So money may be a mitigating factor in the clarity or the truth of what they are saying. A forensic audit of the books of some prophets would lay bare some embarrassing details. However, apart from that, the money side of the story can be an interesting and colourful aspect of the prophet's ministry. It is always possible that a close look at the money side might reveal a story of self-sacrifice and spiritual authenticity.

DON'T...

- Be intimidated by the prophet. He or she may be convinced that God has given the word or may be simply using his or her authoritarian voice to keep the followers in line. As an independent Christian person, watch for signs of demagoguery — authoritarianism that smacks of the implication that the prophet believes he or she is a direct and unique representative of God.

- Write off the prophet. Even the most egotistical, shallow, bombastic or publicity-seeking prophet has a reason for saying what he or she says. Svend Robinson, the gay activist MP from the Vancouver area, loves to talk in the House about his alter ego, Fred Phelps, a fundamentalist Baptist pastor from Kansas City who runs the godhatesfags.com Web site. Yet, even behind Phelps is a basis for what he does — repugnant as it might be — to moderate Christians who want to encourage love, family, life, fellowship, compassion and all that other neat stuff that goes along with being a follower of Jesus. Once the paranoia of the extreme prophet has been peeled away, it can be determined if there is a basis for further consideration.

- Misquote the prophet. Sometimes, in our anxiety to put our own spin on what the prophet has said, we put words in his or her mouth. We do so perhaps because we mistrust the prophet's motivation. Nevertheless, misquoting the prophet can be a low blow that says something about the ethics of the listener. How often have you heard the subject of a news story say, "the reporter decided what the story should be before he ever interviewed me." If the subject is right, then the journalist has something to answer for.

Sometimes it is helpful to get the story behind that which the prophet is trying to communicate. That happened in connection with the above-mentioned Erika Kubassek's questioning of former American president Bill Clinton. Evangelical journalists have been inclined to write off Kubassek's activities because she is so "in your face" and so absolutely certain that she is the only one right. In the case of the Bill Clinton incident, we were able to get a useful and helpful story for *Christian News Ottawa* because my Catholic press gallery colleague, Art Babych, and I each had background information that enabled us to ask questions that would not have occurred to other journalists.

Here is the story that appeared in *CNO* in November 1999:

Activist Gets to Clinton
by Art Babych, with files from Lloyd Mackey

A question about God's role in natural disasters, posed by a reporter for a small Toronto-based Christian newspaper, brought a thoughtful response from United States' president Bill Clinton at a news conference in Ottawa October 8.

Erika Kubassek of Maranatha News *was among a handful of reporters randomly selected by Prime Minister Jean Chrétien to ask a question at the half-hour news confer-*

ence. She wanted to know whether the United States president had given any thought to the question of whether natural disasters were "a message from above that there is moral decay, that there is abortion, that there is violence."

"Actually, I have," Clinton replied. "Particularly because of all the millennial predictions." But he said some of the natural disasters are part of predictable weather patterns "and the others have been predicted for more than a decade now by people who tell us that the climate is warming up.

"The real moral message here is that as we all get richer and use more of the resources God has given us, we're being called upon to take greater care of them," he said. "And I think that we have to deal seriously with the impact of the changing climate."

Clinton noted there is concern over the thinning of the polar ice cap and the consequences it could bring to the whole world.

"So I believe that insofar as these natural disasters are greater in intensity...the primary warning we're getting from on high is that we have to keep — to use the phrase of a person I know reasonably well — we have to keep earth in the balance. We have to respond in an appropriate way."

Kubassek later said that she felt it was important to ask her question of Clinton while linking natural disasters to moral decay, because "the Bible is clear on what happens if they continue on this path."

Kubassek's success was, in fact, a little more than random. An avowed Christian activist on moral matters, she heads a Cambridge-based advocacy organization known as the Moral Support Group.

In order to reach the president, she first arranged with **Maranatha News** *to visit Ottawa as a freelance reporter on* *its behalf, then asked the Parliamentary Press Gallery for a day pass. Once at the Chrétien–Clinton press conference, she sat in the second row of a crowd of journalists numbering some 200.*

There, she was one of about a dozen reporters who succeeded in catching the attention of the prime minister, who moderated the hour-long session.

The American president was in Ottawa to officially open the new United States Embassy and meet with Chrétien.

In retrospect, some observations are worth noting:

- It took at least four Christian journalists to pull this story together: Kubassek herself, Joanna Robertson (editor of *Maranatha News*), Babych, a veteran Hill journalist who took close note of Clinton's reply, and your humble scribe, who was responsible for getting the story into *CNO*.
- The question was asked at a time when much media attention was on Clinton because of his affair with a White House intern, a situation that got him impeached.
- Clinton showed sincere respect for the questioner but, skilled politician that he is, turned the question to make the point he wanted to make: that taking care of the environment is something God asks us to do.

The Clinton presidency was an intriguing paradox. He made no secret of his evangelical Christian faith and regularly sought the advice of such respected Christian leaders as Tony Campolo, Bill Hybels (senior minister of the huge Willow Creek Church near Chicago) and Billy Graham. Yet, the stories about some of Clinton's sexual escapades—a few of which he admitted to when his back was against the wall—had both his supporters and his detractors suggesting that he had a deep-seated sexual addiction.

That particular Ottawa press conference was the second time I had seen Clinton in person. The first was on April 3 and 4, 1993, when he and then Russian president Boris Yeltsin met in a summit in Vancouver.

At the time, Edna and I were members of First Baptist Church, the place Clinton chose to attend on the Sunday morning of April 4. The church was pastored by a venerable Scotsman, Bruce Milne, an exceptional orator and biblical expositor.

While Clinton heard an outstanding sermon that Sunday, Milne's finest moment came in his morning prayer when he functioned movingly and astutely as the American president's "pastor-for-a-day." First, he prayed for Hillary Rodham Clinton, who was visiting her father who lay dying in an Arkansas hospital. Then, he prayed for the unborn and for the mothers who had to make crucial life-and-death decisions. In that moment, he was joining in solidarity with Clinton's own pastor at Immanuel Baptist Church in Little Rock, who had publicly and not entirely gently chided the president for his leanings toward an abortion-on-demand position.

There is no question in my mind that pastors play a crucial role in helping politicians do politics Christianly. They may not always get the hoped-for result, but they have every right to pray for, encourage and even criticize their politician parishioners. They need to know that if the pastor–politician relationship is both compassionate and authentic, it helps more often than not.

In the next chapter, we will take a look at the seeming need of some Christian organizations around the Hill to always have an enemy or an emergency at the ready to successfully fight the war they believe God has given them.

Chapter Eight

The Care and Feeding of Enemies

This chapter introduces some perspective to the next few, where I will:

- Talk about the Christian advocacy spectrum from left to right.
- Explore various Christian approaches to economics.
- Analyze an evangelical funeral through political-coloured glasses.
- Review some of the special challenges that faced Matthew Coon Come when he was grand chief of the Assembly of First Nations.

The centrepiece of this chapter is "doing politics christianly…" #22, which I wrote on May 12, 2001, when I was getting just a little turned off by hearing almost daily about new enemies and emergencies being faced by Christian advocacy organizations.

ENEMIES, EMERGENCIES AND CONFLICT

There were two faith-based events in the capital this week, and both had something to do with violence.

- *The National Prayer Breakfast, pulling together about 700 political, diplomatic, academic and private sector leaders, heard retired Lieutenant-general Roméo Dallaire talk about shaking hands with the devil in Rwanda. As a peacekeeper, he was traumatized during the Rwanda uprising by the futility of trying to stop the slaughter of hundreds of thousands — many of them Christians — killing each other.*
- *The March for Life drew several thousand to Parliament Hill. A friend who is a serious Christian took in the event, initially saying, "So what?" Her thinking was profoundly changed when she heard parliamentary pro-life caucus co-chair, Tory Elsie Wayne, dramatically describe what happens when final trimester abortions are performed. For the first time, my friend felt she could emotionally and spiritually identify with pro-life's objectives.*

While all this was taking place, I recalled some interesting advice about the whole business of enemies, emergencies and conflict. A respected Christian leader, now passed on, once pointed his bony finger at me and said, as closely as I can recall: "Lloyd, you will never raise funds successfully if you don't have either an enemy or an emergency. Better that you have both!"

The implication was that if you have no enemy or emergency, you need to create one. That axiom, for me, caused a fair amount of internal conflict.

Now, as a journalist, I often wonder whether advocacy groups ever stretch or creatively reshape the truth when their marketing people press them to find enemies or emergencies to bolster their fundraising efforts.

The difficulty with creating enemies, particularly,

comes in the necessity of rejecting the option of turning ene-
mies into friends.

A few years ago, I was virtually excommunicated from
the pro-life movement by some of its sterner spokespersons.
The reason for their censure was that I was urging pro-lifers
to reach out to those who are personally opposed to abortion
but ambivalent on the issue of choice. Such reaching out, I
suggested, would prevent many of those people from being
co-opted by the abortion-on-demand folk. My point was that
people are scattered all the way along the life spectrum. Most
people don't like abortion and want it regulated.

My proposition was to urge a common ground on
which the outreach could take place. It was based on the
assumption that it is a laudable social goal to significantly
reduce the number of abortions that take place in our nation.

I believed that people should have the right to help
achieve that goal even if they are ambivalent on some of the
principles on which sanctity of life is based. Further, I opti-
mistically suggested that these "new friends" would lose
their ambivalence if they could see their efforts having at least
some incremental effect.

Just for the record, I have never accepted that I could be
excommunicated from the pro-life movement by a few of its
leaders. Indeed, I still pray, at least occasionally, that Christian
advocates of all types will try to find ways of turning enemies
into friends. It might occasionally foul up the fundraising pro-
cess but reflects, for the most part, the way Jesus did it. True,
he cracked the whip on recalcitrant church leaders, but most
people found him responsive to their needs and desires.

The following paragraphs appeared as an addendum
to the above piece. It took off from the emergency "hook"

and described a particular activity called the "Citizen Project" in which we were engaged at the time at the *Christian News Ottawa* newspaper.

> *Speaking of emergencies: truth to tell, we don't have one, but* Christian News Ottawa, *the church-distributed newspaper published by Christian Info Canada, is placing 85,000 copies next week in* The Ottawa Citizen.
>
> *The issue has been written in such a way as to be of interest to those many people who claim to be Christian or Christian-friendly but don't go to church.*
>
> *Most of our $25,000 in costs related to the issue are being covered by advertising. If a dozen or so of our several hundred readers could contribute somewhere between $100 and $500 each, we would be able to pay all the related bills. Christian Info Canada is a registered charity and can issue a charitable receipt for tax purposes.*
>
> *Thanks for your prayers and interest.*

I hope this piece has been helpful as food for thought before plowing into the mental recreation of the next few chapters.

Chapter Nine

Advocacy Here and There

In this chapter, we take a look at the advocacy done by two different Christian groups, Citizens for Public Justice (CPJ) and Canada Family Action Coalition. The former works from a social justice perspective; the latter works for political action in the pro-family area, with a significant sideline involving religious freedom.

In "doing politics christianly..." #37, written on August 27, 2001, we introduce CPJ through the personage of its founder, Gerald Vandezande, on the occasion of his having been inducted into the Order of Canada.

CALL TO ORDER FOR GERALD VANDEZANDE

The periodic Order of Canada appointment announcements often represent an effective antidote to the argument that the Christian faith – particularly in its evangelical form – has been marginalized in Canadian society.

This week, there were several appointments to membership in the Order that caught the interest of this particular watchful eye; among them was Gerald Vandezande.

Vandezande has worked in a vocation in which his

113

Christian faith was an integral part of the job description. He joins a list of about 4,000 Canadians who have been honoured since 1967 in twice-annual ceremonies at Rideau Hall in Ottawa by whoever was the governor-general at the time.

The ceremony, the particular designation, plus the wording of the citation that describes the reason for the honour are all the end result of a complex nomination and decision-making process.

The Order of Canada appears to be as good a way as any to publicly honour Canadians who have contributed positively in whatever field engaged them. In addition, serious Christians have their fair share of the honours.

Vandezande's order citation describes him as a "powerful and respected voice for social justice." He was a founding member of Citizens for Public Justice and worked there for thirty-five years, first as executive director and latterly as national public affairs director. CPJ was founded mainly by Dutch immigrants connected with churches that usually have "Reformed" in their names.

Education and labour were the main themes of those Dutch-spawned concerns in the early years. Vandezande, originally a banker and cost accountant, entered the Christian social justice field through the labour "door" as executive secretary of the Christian Labour Association of Canada — one of the institutions always a part of the Reformed culture. Another, of course, is the Christian school. Under Vandezande, CPJ found it natural to seek "public justice" for both those areas. The list grew through the years to include aboriginal rights and an "economy of care." That latter sentiment expanded into activity connected with refugee concerns and child poverty.

The list of organizations with which Vandezande has networked shows how skilfully he has worked from the basis

of his own core faith without being afraid to wade into rela-
tionships with groups that were theologically different and
instead sharing interest in similar justice themes.

He has been active in both the Christian Reformed
Church and the Evangelical Fellowship of Canada. Those
groups reflect his basic faith perspective. He has been
involved in such other groups as the Ecumenical Working
Group on Abortion Policy, the Ontario Multi-Faith
Coalition for Equity in Education and the Interfaith Working
Group on Canada's Future.

It is hard to politically pigeonhole Vandezande. Some
see him as a religious conservative and economic leftist. That
he has consistently called on government and the corporate
community to repent for actions and policies of injustice is
seen as fair evidence of that mix. That he attempts to inte-
grate a God-shaped view into his pronouncements provides
some explanation for what some, particularly on the social or
economic right, might see as a conundrum.

His encouragement of the concept of "registered domestic
partnerships" as one way for governments to create an alterna-
tive to marriage without marginalizing the traditional family
was one example of such a justice-motivated conundrum.

In chapter fifteen, we will look at several Christian
people who have been honoured with the Order of Canada,
with a view to examining how their Christian faith helped
them to achieve what they did to merit the honour.

The next piece, "doing politics christianly..." #20,
written April 28, 2001, provides comparison and contrast
for purposes of noting that there is more than one viewpoint from which Christians advocate—and more than
one issue on which to legitimately advocate.

We will also take a careful look at the advocacy issue as it impacted the first Canadian Alliance leadership campaign. This is a subject that, even at this late date, still stirs up Christian sensitivities.

Who is More Pro-Life, Pro-Family?

An intriguing factor in the recent Canadian Alliance leadership dust-up involves the ways in which Christian pro-life and pro-family groups communicate their views to the politicians.

Last year, when a Commons committee debated a bill extending certain benefits and pensions to same-sex couples, five press releases arrived in my e-mail at the end of each committee hearing day.

For simplicity's sake, I will deal with two releases. One, from the Evangelical Fellowship of Canada (EFC), took a firm but carefully-worded stance that marriage is the exclusive domain of one man and one woman. The other, from Canada Family Action Coalition (CFAC), was much more toughly worded.

The EFC operates within the presupposition that it brings the deeply held values of its members to pluralism's table. By contrast, CFAC tends to identify its enemies clearly and speaks much more bluntly in expressing its pro-life and pro-family stances.

The CFAC's enemy-identifying strategy came into play in the Canadian Alliance leadership race. Early on, CFAC president Roy Beyer separated himself from the organization to form a group known as Families for Day. He worked loosely in tandem with other institutions such as Canada Christian College (CCC) and Ontario Christian Herald

(OCH) newspaper to encourage Christians to join the CA and support Stockwell Day's leadership bid.

Many people worked quietly to get pro-life and pro-family candidates to run for the CA. In some ridings, these people were reported to have indicated that the best kinds of pro-family and pro-life Christians were those who supported Day over Preston Manning.

Day's supporters insisted that while Preston Manning was just as committed an evangelical Christian as Day, he was less accessible to pro-life and pro-family groups.

After Day won the CA leadership, the Families for Day, CCC and OCH let it be known that they were proud of having made a difference in the leadership race.

All the above came to mind earlier this week [April 2001] as Ian Todd resigned as Day's chief of staff, Alliance MPs Deborah Grey, Chuck Strahl and Grant McNally quit their shadow cabinet posts and MP Art Hanger urged Day to resign the CA leadership.

Now, Day, Manning, Todd, Grey, Strahl, McNally and Hanger all have something in common. They are all evangelical Christians, and their Christian faith, in every case, extends to clear support for pro-life and pro-family issues. (An interesting aside: Grey, Strahl and McNally are alumni of Trinity Western University [TWU], an increasingly significant institution in the development of Canadian Christian leaders.)

I submit that the tension between pro-Day and pro-Manning Christians is that Day is seen – whether justified or not – as too beholden to the kind of pro-life and pro-family advocacy that sees identifying the enemy as good political strategy.

Let's examine one example of the potential for tension.

Commenting on Ian Todd's resignation, Lifesite News, a pro-life e-mail news service, suggested that Todd's previous work as a key aide to Preston Manning demonstrated that he was the reason Manning was relatively inaccessible to pro-life and pro-family groups.

Lifesite *did not reveal that Todd's father-in-law and Manning had been instrumental in leading Todd to a vibrant Christian faith in recent years, and that faith included a strong sense of servanthood to both the political bosses he worked for.*

True, Manning had a different way of listening to and articulating pro-life and pro-family views — an approach more in line with EFC strategies. Todd facilitated Manning's communication style.

The faith-based tension surrounding the two Canadian Alliance leadership races are mostly in the background now. While it would be an exaggeration to say that all is smooth sailing, many of the Christians involved in the conflicts have agreed to not keep the fight going.

Manning is doing valuable work "scouting" out new talent and ways of politically doing things. His book, *Think Big,* deserves recognition as a contemporary political ethics text. With the wisdom of years, he will be able to use his faith-based reconciliation skills to build the kind of coalitions needed to keep Canada hanging together (old joke: otherwise we will hang separately). Much of that could happen through think-tanking — particularly with the Manning Centre for Building Democracy.

Day is a very competent foreign affairs critic who has learned to listen to a wide variety of people, including all kinds of Christian internationalists, in the pursuit of his portfolio's objectives. Although he has never asked me, I would tell him that as long as he is prepared to listen carefully to what Manning has to say, he will grow as a believer, a person and a politician. Day is a good quick study. He can be very kind and warm, but he has a steely edge to him.

One of Day's most valuable contributions to Canadian politics has been his biblically-spawned relationship building with the conservative Jewish community.

Chuck Strahl, mentioned earlier, made good use of his experience in "exile" from the CA as deputy leader of the PC-DR parliamentary coalition. There, he worked closely for seven months with then Tory leader Joe Clark and his successor, Peter MacKay. Now, as deputy speaker, he is making extensive use of his conciliation skills.

I am sorry that Deb Grey has chosen to leave politics, especially as it seems, on the surface, that her protagonist, Day, survived and she did not. In the view of at least one Christian journalist, Licia Corbella, editor of the *Calgary Sun*, Grey and the other "dissidents" helped save the CA. Grey's own particular role was to permit herself to be interviewed for an article that Regent College professor and long-time Alberta political analyst Maxine Hancock wrote for *ChristianWeek*.

I know many of my friends who are Day supporters would argue with me, but my modest view is that Hancock nailed both the leadership and faith issues firmly in the piece she did. I hope that in due course, as part of the healing process, Day will be able to thank Grey for rescuing him from the abyss some of his supporters were creating for him and giving him a second chance to "do it right."

The next piece, written on July 3, 2001, weaves in the advocacy approach of Citizens Research Institute, run by a BC activist dynamo named Kari Simpson. It introduces some of the details of the Trinity Western case as a means of drawing a line between advocacy and education in the Christian and political context.

ADVOCACY AND EDUCATION—DRAWING THE LINES WITH CARE

A few days ago, writing for the Globe and Mail, *Ian Hunter suggested that the Supreme Court decision in favour of Trinity Western University might not provide quite as much reason for rejoicing as has been previously indicated. He is one of several respected Christian writers and thinkers who make the point that, while the court protects the rights of Christians to believe what they do, it does not leave much room for them to convert that belief into behaviour. (TWU's conflict was with the British Columbia College of Teachers over religious freedom and gay rights issues.)*

Hunter is a man whose shoes I would be unworthy to unloose. A distinguished law professor emeritus at the University of Western Ontario, he possesses a finely honed, Christianly shaped legal mind. Having said that, I would like to suggest that he is leaving some things unsaid in order to make his point.

Since arriving on the Hill three years ago, I have learned a bit about advocacy groups, political parties...and Christian universities. I come to the subject with a vested interest. For many years, one of my spare-time activities was teaching business and communications subjects at Trinity Western. I have a personal regard for the school that grows out of an acquired respect for many of its key people.

Trinity Western handled the case precisely in the way a Christian university should. At the time the story first emerged, there was an overture to help from at least one family-issue advocacy group. Kari Simpson, head of the BC-based Citizens Research Council, told me at the time that she thought that Trinity should "go political" on the issue. She was disappointed that the university's leaders and legal counsel gently declined her offer of help.

Some advocacy groups, on both the left and the right, tend to overstate their case to make their point. In so doing, they make effective use of drama, satire and sarcasm. Christian advocacy groups are often not much different from their secular counterparts in the methods they use to make their points. Advocacy groups may also use marches, pickets and, perhaps, limited civil disobedience to ensure the media carries their message. All these means of attention-getting and point-making get people who are on the other sides of the issues angry. They sometimes create division among Christians, as understandable tensions develop over whose message is best heard. There can even be a certain meanness and arrogance – unintended or otherwise – to the measures taken by advocates, directed toward those Christians who have not fallen in completely with their viewpoint.

Advocacy leaders will argue that what they do is an essential part of their success and that such groups have an important role in advancing certain Christian causes and agendas. "If you don't shout loud enough," they will say, "nobody will listen."

Point taken. But wisdom calls for a clear delineation between the roles of Christian advocacy groups and Christian universities.

The TWU court decision came just a few months short of the fortieth anniversary of the founding of what is now Trinity Western University. It reflected a tacit recognition that Christian universities have historically helped

Christians make wise and informed contributions to society.

When Trinity Western was founded in 1962 as Trinity Junior College, the leaders in its sponsoring denomination, the Evangelical Free Church, struggled with whether it should be a Bible school or a liberal arts college. Advocates for the latter prevailed, thanks to a clear recognition that Protestant universities in Canada were being rapidly secularized. (The last to go was Waterloo Lutheran, which became Wilfrid Laurier about thirty years ago.)

A Christian university is at the forefront of a maturing Christian community. It helps its community develop in a manner that gives impact to the surrounding society, while preserving the spiritual values that give that same community its vigour and substance.

In those years since 1962, several other Protestant Christian universities have emerged and more show every sign of doing so. The ones already out in the open are Canadian Mennonite, Atlantic Baptist and St. Stephen's. Each has a different history and has emerged from a different faith culture.

Some of the others headed the same way are Briercrest, Providence, King's, Redeemer and Tyndale. Likewise, they have a variety of histories. Some come from evangelical roots, others from reformed. Some have spent most of their existence as Bible colleges, emerging only more recently as Christian liberal arts schools. Others are university colleges now moving into full flower. (There are other instances, of course, of evangelical Christian graduate schools affiliated with secular universities, such as Regent at UBC and Wycliffe at the University of Toronto. But that is another story.)

All these schools face a range of pressures. As they move to push the intellectual and social envelopes within their communities, they create regret in the minds of those who feel they are "departing from the Word." Conversely, when they maintain community, in a biblically acceptable way that contrasts with society's relatively greater diversity, they are seen as a threat to the outside world.

Often, the role of a Christian university is to establish with its alumni the confidence to speak with integrity, clarity and intelligence on provocative issues. Indeed, given the necessary time, it can help prepare advocacy groups to forward their causes in ways that generate lots of light without too much heat.

So, what does all this have to do with Trinity Western and Ottawa? Well, not too long from now, Trinity Western will have a second address. It is in Ottawa, just a few blocks from the Hill. The university has been able to acquire a 100-year-old heritage home. The motivation to do so comes from TWU's graduate school dean, Don Page, whose dream of an Ottawa presence has burned quietly for the past decade. That was when he moved west from Ottawa, where he had been a senior policy advisor to such foreign affairs ministers as Mitchell Sharp and Joe Clark and where he was the spirit behind a vibrant Public Service Christian Fellowship that involved hundreds of civil servants in weekly Bible studies.

Not much is publicly said, yet, about this development, because some of the pieces are still being put in place. The best way to learn more is to check the Trinity Western Web page and watch for more news toward fall. From here, it is an encouraging development that will have considerable impact in the next few years on the way in which Canadian Christian universities will bring informed and effective perspectives to bear, for the good of both advocacy and politics.

Lloyd Mackey

That heritage home to which I refer did, indeed, become Laurentian Leadership Centre of Trinity Western University. The next story provides a little more of the colour and detail about this new/old Ottawa institution.

LAURENTIAN CENTRE: READY FOR LEADERSHIP

At last count, twenty-two Trinity Western University senior students are taking up residence in a century-old red brick mansion now known as Laurentian Leadership Centre, just blocks from Parliament Hill.

They represent the fulfillment of the dream Donald Page had when he moved west twelve years ago after being a senior policy advisor to foreign affairs ministers Mitchell Sharp and Joe Clark.

Page, graduate studies dean at TWU based in Langley, near Vancouver, envisaged a place where future Christian leaders could get a taste of the nation's capital while pursuing studies in such fields as international relations, political science and communications.

In the spring of 2001, the "right building" was identified. It was the former Laurentian Club that, in its early years, was the home of the Booth family of timber barons. Trinity acquired it for a reported $1.8 million and began extensive renovations while preserving its heritage character. The four-storey, 18,000 square foot, finely finished mansion at 252 Metcalfe Street is about a ten-minute walk from Parliament Hill.

The twenty-two students will each spend one or two semesters at the Centre. They will take senior level undergrad studies in leadership, public policy and law/government. All of them have internships on the Hill. International relations and political science students are assigned to members of Parliament, some of them cabinet ministers; those in communications will relate to print and electronic media that are part of the Parliamentary Press Gallery.

Ready to work with them are Paul Wilson and Sheldon Loeppky, Laurentian's program director and student life coordinator, respectively. For several years in the late nineties, Wilson was research director for the official opposition on the Hill. His Ph.D. in history is from Queen's University, where he studied under the eminent evangelical historian, the late George Rawlyk. Loeppky, who is on the student life staff at Trinity's Langley campus, will establish that program at Laurentian before returning west in 2003.

Wilson will be teaching the leadership course. Bruce Clemenger, director of Evangelical Fellowship of Canada's Ottawa-based Centre for Public Policy, will handle that assignment. The law and government teacher will be announced soon.

According to Page, the establishing of an Ottawa presence has been part of the maturing process of the university. The school, which began in 1962 on a Fraser Valley former dairy farm, has evolved from a two-year junior college with seventeen students to full university status and its attendant graduate studies, with an enrolment closing in on 3,500. Neil Snider, its president since the mid-seventies, holds the distinction of being the longest-serving Canadian university chief. The school's roots are in the Evangelical Free Church, but it draws its enrolment from a wide range of religious backgrounds.

TWU was in the national picture in the late nineties and 2000, when its conflict with the British Columbia College of Teachers over religious freedom and gay rights

125

issues was working its way through to the Supreme Court of Canada. Trinity won its case at the supreme and appeal court levels in BC before moving to the top court.

The end result of the Supreme Court ruling in its favour was that Trinity was permitted to establish its own self-standing teacher education faculty. The BCCT had maintained that the school's community standards, which required student commitment to refrain from extra-marital heterosexual and homosexual activity, could cause the teachers it educated to discriminate against homosexual young people.

The grand-opening activities for the Laurentian Centre will take place in early October [2002]. Preston Manning, former leader of the opposition, will address a gala at the Chateau Laurier Hotel on October 10.

The grand opening took place, and each semester introduces the political world of Ottawa to a new set of students. Watch for word that some of these students eventually emerge as federal politicians. There might even be a few cabinet ministers among them.

Chapter Ten

Learning from the Christian Left

One of the frustrations of evangelical Christians who are unable to buy into a left-leaning vision of economics is that they find it hard to locate someone who articulates a biblical basis for free enterprise, personal initiative and market economics with the kind of seeming compassion that left-leaning Christians exhibit.

Bill Phipps, the United Church moderator from 1998 to 2000, is perhaps best remembered for his suggestion that he was not sure Jesus was God. However, he did know for sure that the markets were not God. He expressed this conviction during his legacy-making last year in office, when he set up a round of sessions across Canada through which he helped church members explore the relationship between social justice and economics. His last session attracted about 200 participants to one of the committee rooms in the Parliament Buildings, where a host of panellists and speakers worked at the subject for two days.

Phipps' parliamentary session was a superb piece of work for his particular viewpoint. I recall how he emphasized that those who trust in the markets rather than working for economic justice are idolaters because the market economic system is their god.

In the narrowest sense, what he said was beyond argument. But his logic could have been tackled by suggesting that many left-leaning Christians are idolaters as well because they treat the environment as though it is a god.

In my modest view, what needed explanation was the "unseen hand" to which right-leaning economists often refer. Both the environment and the economy can be seen as creations of God. Thus it is important that Christians try to understand both the economy and the environment in the God context. In doing so, they can try to find ways in which a reliance on the God of the environment and the God of the economy can bring more justice, better conditions and less repression to humankind.

Left-leaning Christians speak of being stewards of God's environment. Yet, when they see people trying to understand the workings of the "unseen hand" touted by right-wing economists as the product of a caring God, they protest. It seems to become a control issue.

That, then, was the frustration I faced after listening carefully to the Phipps session.

Some of what I would like to see happen in the area of Christian influence on politics is in the area of economics. The "doing politics christianly..." piece written on June 2, 2001 helped to crystallize some of the paradigm shift available for Christian economists and fiscally-oriented politicians to address. This column talks about Hernando DeSoto and Walter Block in a context that I hope is helpful.

THE MYSTERY AND THE MISERY

Just a few inches from the laptop on which I am typing are several books I often refer to: Holy Bible *(Amsterdam '86 edition),* Canadian Press Style Book, Ontario Christian Resource Directory, The Seven Habits of Highly Effective People *by Stephen Covey and* Lausanne Occasional Paper #24: Co-operating in World Evangelization—a Handbook on Church/Para-church Relationships *by Keith Price.*

Price passed away shortly after I wrote this piece, but his book is a modern classic and has been reprinted for future Christian leaders to consider.

There is one more book: Morality of the Market: Religious and Economic Perspectives, *one of whose editors is Walter Block.*

I got to know Block in the eighties when he was heading up the Centre for Religion and Economics under the aegis of the Fraser Institute, a right-leaning economic think-tank in Vancouver. He later went to teach at a Catholic college in New England, and I lost track of him. I have often wondered, in recent years, where Walter Block was now that we needed him.

Shortly after writing this piece, I received word that Block was teaching at Duke University in North Carolina.

Block's reason for starting the Centre was simple enough. He grew weary, Sabbath by Sabbath, of hearing his rabbi enunciate left-wing solutions to the issues of oppression and poverty. In that, he was at one with the many Christians who wish they could find modern-day prophets who can draw from the great themes of individual initiative, property owner-

ship and free enterprise that are woven through the pages of Holy Writ. It is easy enough, Block contended, to find bishops, pastors and rabbis who can enunciate the social gospel and social justice, with nary a reference to the other side of the coin.

I thought of Block again recently, when I wrote about former United Church moderator Robert Smith's seemingly prophetic utterances against free trade, just prior to the Quebec City Americas summit. His comments were the subject of "doing politics christianly..." #19, entitled "The Misery of My People," covered in chapter two.

As stated earlier, Smith was particularly strong about what he saw to be the failings of free trade. He spoke of the Mexican border city of Ciudad Juarez, home to 397 maquila factories employing 281,000 workers who assemble electronics products and car parts for export to the United States and Canada. His point was that in this city, whose free-trade zone status predates NAFTA by twenty-five years, it took three factory jobs to maintain one family in a cardboard shack. I reported newly elected Mexican President Vicente Fox's rather mild response that it takes time for the benefits of free trade to work their way through the population.

All that was written before I started reading The Mystery of Capital, *by Hernando de Soto, a Peruvian economist who has directed serious research on capital and property issues in such cities as Port-au-Prince, Cairo and Manila.*

A major thesis of the book is that, in places such as Canada, the United States and many other "Western" nations, the right to ownership of property is a given, protected by an almost invisible but long-established regimen of laws and practices. That regimen, he says, is a major key to the relative prosperity enjoyed by most of our populations.

What is taken for granted here is almost unknown in Latin America, large parts of Africa and the former communist countries of Europe and Asia.

Examples?

- *It took six hours a day for almost a year to fill out all the forms and paperwork involved in starting a small garment workshop, near Lima, employing one worker.*
- *In Egypt it takes from five to fourteen years of bureaucratic back-and-forthing to start one legal business.*

All this had me head-scratching. Were not many Latin American and African nations strongly influenced, both traditionally and in recent years, by the church and by Christian missions, relief and development activity?

In de Soto's view, religion and culture, debt relief and foreign aid do not have much to do with what he is talking about. Very simply, it is a question of "dead capital." Millions of people who moved from rural settings into teeming cities over the past two or three decades do not own the property on which they live, play and work. Not owning it, they cannot raise capital, either through credit or the attracting of investment.

When they cannot raise capital, they are unable to expand to produce the goods and services necessary to a healthy society, take on employees, care for their families or act in a spirit of entrepreneurship

Twelve years ago, I felt just a little of what de Soto is talking about when my brother, Barry Mackey, at the time a micro-enterprise specialist with Christian Children's Fund of Canada, introduced me to a community worker from Haiti. The Haitian asked me many questions about how he could start a Christian newspaper in his home nation.

Lloyd Mackey

I really did not know where to start, because all the capital and infrastructure issues I could take for granted had no equivalency in Haiti. Who could buy advertising? No one. So there was no way to pay for printing. Who would invest or seed the project if they could see no way it could continue toward self-sufficiency? Same answer, pretty much.

Having now read a fair chunk of The Mystery of Capital, *I begin to get some sense that there is even more at stake here than the mere means to sell advertising and pay the printer.*

This book will not sit well with many Christian leaders who have invested their lives in trying to close the gap between rich and poor. Whether they look at a transforming personal gospel or the advocacy of social justice – or both – as the means to meet deep human needs, they may well see The Mystery *as a simplistic, one-issue approach.*

Donner Canadian Foundation advisor Patrick Luciani, writing about the book in The National Post *on May 24 [2001], recognized the potential dichotomy. While he did not comment on the adequacy or otherwise of traditional evangelical missiology, he provocatively questioned the approach of Quebec City anti-globalization protestors, some of who would identify, in part at least, with the "liberation theology" advocated by Robert Smith.*

"Will the protestors in Barcelona, Quebec City and Seattle get behind the idea of real land reform by advocating that the poor get legal title to their land, apartments and houses?" he asked, answering rhetorically: "Not likely. They seem more intent on restricting trade, disrupting capital flows, raising taxes and shutting down poverty conferences."

Strong words. Not the kind I would use, but I could certainly identify with one of Walter Block's heroes, Catholic philosopher Michael Novak. He believes that many oft-ignored answers to oppression and poverty lie in the concepts of capitalism that can be shaped – rather than shredded – by a compassionate Christian gospel.

Another bit of reading worth exploring comes from doing a Web search of Robin Richardson and/or Fraser Institute. Richardson's name pops up every few years on the Canadian scene. He was a senior economist at a major commercial bank in the seventies when he experienced a serious conversion to Christ. He left banking to become a Tory MP, serving only in the short-lived government of Joe Clark in 1979–80.

Shortly after, he spent serious time in theological and economics graduate studies in the United States, in a high-level quest to integrate his views on economics and his growing Christian faith. For a while after that, he pastored a church in Victoria, then set up a retreat house for Canadian Forces personnel from nearby CFB Esquimalt.

Richardson also did major research and writing work on the subject of international and Canadian public debt, under the auspices of the right-wing economic think-tank, the Fraser Institute. Many economists see his work as having been seminal to the effort of the Reform Party under Preston Manning to keep debt reduction on the public agenda. The practical outcome was, as it often is with Liberal regimes, that the government did what the opposition said should be done. Within a few years, then finance minister Paul Martin had moved annual budgets from a deficit to a surplus position, and the national debt began to come down. In the process, Martin became known as a fiscal conservative, even though his deficit-cutting policies were much more reliant on raising taxes than on cutting spending — as Preston Manning would have wished.

As for Richardson, he seems to have some strong awareness that being a Christian and a fiscal conservative is no oxymoron. Yet, the living out of his Christian faith is alternatively focused on social, fiscal and spiritual action. It is almost as if there are three Robin Richardsons in play. One is obvious for a few years, then another shows up. They are not contradictory — they simply work out that way.

In the run-up to the 2000 election, Richardson decided try for a Canadian Alliance nomination. Instead of running in a riding where he might have a better chance as a fiscal conservative — in Victoria or Saanich — he tackled popular physician Keith Martin, then a CA MP who had been the most liberal of the candidates for the party's first leadership race. Martin later jumped to the Liberals.

Richardson ran against him on a social conservative platform, believing that presented a clear challenge to Martin, who was pretty much at the pro-choice end of the spectrum, at least a far as a Catholic could afford to be without having to leave the fold.

So, in that sense, we still await someone who can be a Michael Novak, who can really integrate a biblical understanding of an economically interested God with a willingness to make fiscal conservatism work his purposes.

Could Stephen Harper be such a person? He declined to make it an issue when he ran in Calgary Southwest, following his election to the CA leadership. His major opponent was the aforementioned Bill Phipps, who still holds a United Church pulpit in Calgary. Phipps wanted to engage Harper in a major economic debate, but Harper wouldn't bite. I was disappointed, because I thought Harper would have done very well against Phipps, thoroughly formed economist that he is. I have seen him defend his fiscal conservatism against economic socialist activists, and he is superb.

Harper may not have felt confident, however, that the integration of his own faith with a debatable economic stance could stand up to an old hand like Phipps. After all, the former United Church moderator has previously demonstrated that he can make denial of the deity of Jesus sound like a deeply compassionate and spiritual idea.

So my wait continues. But that might be all right. One of the elements of the political right that comes out time after time is the belief that individual initiative trumps state control. On that basis, perhaps it is better that Richardson continue to live out his faith in whatever way he should and simply bring that faith-based fiscal conservative thinking to the political table on call. After all, he would be creating yet another conundrum if he tried to persuade the government to unduly control free enterprise and the "unseen hand" in the interests of making it all more "Christian." If he were to take that course of action, he would come exceedingly close to Bill Phipps' way of doing things.

Chapter Eleven

Two Funerals: Both Christian, Both Political

Funerals are good places to get a measure of the cultures surrounding various faith and culture groups. They help to explain what goes on in a culture that defines where the "insiders" get their motivation and how they relate — or try to freeze out — the outsiders.

Later in this chapter, I will tell you about a "really good" evangelical funeral, one that had all the strongly emotional elements of evangelical faith/sports/politics culture.

First, however, I want to share an excerpt from my book *Like Father, Like Son: Ernest Manning and Preston Manning.* This piece contrasts two political funerals that took place just a few months apart. One marked the death of Ernest Manning, the other of Joe Ghiz, who was the Liberal premier of Prince Edward Island.

At the time of writing this book, I happened to watch the live coverage on "CBC Newsworld" of the funeral of Joe Ghiz, premier of Prince Edward Island during the last half of the 1980s. The son of Lebanese immigrants, Ghiz was a brilliant orator whose place on the national stage came during the Charlottetown Accord talks, during which he eloquently defended both Canadian unity and what he perceived to be Quebec's special place within Canada.

The similarities and contrasts between the funerals of Joe Ghiz and Ernest Manning were both striking and significant. Each drew about 1,200 people. Ghiz's state ecumenical funeral took place in the gothic splendour of 100-year-old St. Dunstan's Basilica on a tree-lined downtown Charlottetown street and was attended by Prime Minister Chrétien. The officiating clergymen were gowned. The liturgies of Canada's mainstream churches – Catholic and Anglican – were studiously followed. Ghiz's widow, mother, daughter and son sat quietly in the front row. References to the relationship between Ghiz's faith and political life were implicit. The eulogy included a reference to times at the family cottage when – a good cigar in hand and couple of Scotches and a barbecued steak under his belt – Joe would regale the gathered clan with warmly told political tales.

And there was some speculation that Ghiz's university-student son might follow in his father's political footsteps.

By contrast, Ernest Manning's funeral was in the sleek, windowless fifteen-year-old First Alliance Church in suburban Calgary. The ministers wore business suits. The only federal politicians in sight were Reform MPs. The service exuded evangelical informality and included eulogies from Manning's son Preston and one of his granddaughters, lawyer Andrea Manning Kroon. She noted, "For us kids, Grandpa was our source of history, knowledge and understanding of life, love, relationships, achievement, business, law and politics – just by watching him and talking to him." His serious commitment to balancing faith and political action was made clear.

Manning's funeral did not get live play on the CBC. It was videotaped and later run on "100 Huntley Street," the Christian talk show hosted by Pentecostal communicator David Mainse. Preston Manning's eulogy ran in full in the Globe and Mail.

However, the similarities between the funerals were just as intriguing as the differences. Both services were strongly Christian, biblical and emotionally moving.

Particularly striking at Ghiz's service was the choice of Scripture, especially a passage from John's gospel noting, in Jesus' words, "I am the way and the truth and the life. No one comes to the Father except through me" (John 14:6).

That passage affirms in the strongest terms the evangelical verity that was part of Ernest Manning's faith – the uniqueness of Jesus among the world's religious leaders. Christian theologians have argued for centuries that the ability of Christians to live by Christian values rests in their personal commitment to God the Son. That, in essence, was Manning's message each week on the "National Bible Hour," every year for fifty years. The two funerals help to define, in some sense at least, the east–west solitudes with which Ernest Manning dealt and in which Preston Manning finds himself.

Prince Edward Island is old Canadian establishment, where Europeans settled and brought their culture long before Confederation. Alberta did not become a province until 1905. Most of the European settlement did not begin until the turn of the century in that province. Furthermore, the discovery of oil began a new, technologically-driven era of development.

Christianity has been and continues to be an influence in Canada, but its expression is often shaped by the predominant culture of each region. The cultural factors result in a range of emphases, with Christianity taking on different hues in different places.

Ernest Manning emphasized the individual side of faith. It was thus consistent for him to stress less government and more individual responsibility. He spoke often about the life-changing effect of commitment to Jesus Christ. He wanted his listeners to understand that their parents, church or good works could not make them Christians. As individuals, they were responsible for their own spiritual condition and destiny.

In the longer-established mainline churches predominant in eastern Canada, there is more emphasis on the importance of the Christian community in shaping the individual. Parents are reminded that, when children are brought for baptism, church and family enter into a contract to spiritually nurture those offspring.

In both paradigms, however, there is another side of the picture. In the evangelical churches that played such an important part in Ernest Manning's life, there is, behind the emphasis on individual responsibility, a strong sense of community. Conversely, in the established churches where community is emphasized, there is a muted, nevertheless distinct, acceptance of the importance of the individual.

The comparison/contrast process for analyzing the Ghiz and Manning funerals helps sort out the leverage provided by the individual and community emphases.

Before visiting another evangelical funeral, I want to touch on the contrasting media coverage of the two funerals — particularly the way in which CBC "covers" Canadian funerals of consequence.

That the Ghiz rites merited state status and subsequent coverage by the government-owned television system is understandable from an historic perspective. However, because Catholicism is so dominant in some parts of central and eastern Canada, it is then a given that Catholic funerals related to significant events and personalities get the whole nine yards.

The Ghiz funeral was a case in point. The two others worth noting were the service for forty-two people from a Quebec town who died in a bus accident and the rites for Pierre Elliott Trudeau.

In all three instances, the presence of what irreverently might be called "play-by-play" and "colour commentary" were present in the form of priests or other church spokespersons who could explain what was going on to the liturgically deprived.

To this point, coverage of evangelical persons of significance does not yet rate. (I could stand corrected if I could see the tapes of Baptist John Diefenbaker's funeral. He was the closest to an evangelical that Canada has had in the prime minister's chair since fellow-Baptist Alexander Mackenzie in the late nineteenth century.)

Understand, please: I am not really complaining. The sociology makes sense. It helps to sort out the sect/church mindset that we dealt with earlier.

THE YLI-RENKO MACMILLAN PATERSON CONNECTION

Today's "doing politics christianly..." was going to be about politics, of course. What else is new? After all, Ottawa is about politics.

Then Edna and I went to a funeral yesterday afternoon. Like many evangelical funerals, it was more of a celebration. Tears and laughter flowed freely together. There was a strong

Lloyd Mackey

sense of community within the crowd of 500, though they ranged in age from tiny children to octogenarians. The singing of "It is Well with My Soul," "The Old Rugged Cross" and "Because He Lives," strong with harmony and emotion, sent shivers up and down my spine.

Pastor Al MacMillan of the Bridlewood Community Church of the Nazarene in Kanata, Ottawa's high-tech suburb, preached. He quietly talked of resurrection and hope and knowing Jesus personally. He described the difference between biblical and contemporary hope with this illustration: "I have a friend," he said, "who hopes that the Toronto Maple Leafs will win the Stanley Cup...some day." Biblical hope, however, he said, is more an expression of certainty.

The funeral was that of Colleen Sue Yli-Renko, born in 1959. She died last week [June 2001] of cancer.

Colleen was a businessperson extraordinaire, a mother whose two daughters loved her willingness to "shop 'til you drop," and the spouse of Kari, a man who played football for the Chicago Bears, Ottawa Roughriders, Toronto Argonauts and Hamilton Tigercats.

Kari and Colleen were a sort of Christian power couple – in the best sense of the word – around Ottawa. They were part of a small group of footballers from the United States who ended up in Canada through the CFL. After retiring from the game, Kari worked with Larry Brune, a former Roughrider from Texas, in the development of the Lone Star Café chain. More recently, they encouraged a range of Christian leadership and ministry initiatives around the nation's capital. At times they scratched their heads over the fact that God placed them in this insular Europeanish city that makes mincemeat of so many who dare to bend its rules.

Colleen not only won Kari's heart when they were both university students in Ohio, she also led him to Jesus.

When Al MacMillan preached her funeral sermon, he carried out her wishes in extending the invitation to those among the gathered who did not yet know Jesus to respond to his calling. MacMillan did it without pressure or manipulation, quietly and with dignity. Five people responded. To Colleen, undoubtedly looking down over the heavenly parapets, that was good. One believer had gone to heaven. Now, there were five more to continue her earthly work.

I only talked to Colleen twice in my life. She was an advertiser in Christian News Ottawa. *She operated a children's play place called Gym Jam. She knew marketing and business planning, and her colleagues recall that she understood human relationships—all within the context of a warm and vibrant Christian faith.*

There is some good faith/politics networking stuff in this story, as well.

Larry Brune and Kari Yli-Renko keep a close eye on the Christian Embassy, a Campus Crusade ministry that sets up Bible study groups for diplomats and parliamentarians. CE is one of several Christian ministries in and around the Hill, and they tend to complement each other. They represent that part of the Christian community that provides some pastoral care to the politicians who spend a lot of time away from their home ridings and spiritual roots.

The other major "subset" is the cluster of Christian organizations that offer counsel on public policy matters— groups such as the Evangelical Fellowship of Canada, the Canadian Conference of Catholic Bishops, Canada Family Action Coalition, the Centre for Cultural Renewal, the Mennonite Central Committee... the list goes on.

Let me wrap, however, with a few more words about Al MacMillan and his wife, Goldie.

The Fraser Valley riding in British Columbia has, for the past three decades, produced MPs whose Christian leadership skills were already being practised before they went into federal politics.

The CA's Chuck Strahl was preceded by Ross Belsher of the Conservatives. They were both lay leaders in their respective Christian and Missionary Alliance churches in Chilliwack and Abbotsford. It should be noted that the transition from Tory to Reform in 1993 in that riding was a credit to the integrity of both men.

Belsher, in turn, had succeeded the late Alex Paterson, a Nazarene pastor who represented the riding for Social Credit and, later, the Tories. He was a strong, quiet man like his son-in-law, Al MacMillan, husband of Goldie. So quiet, in fact, that people anxious to succeed him often plotted to topple him on the basis that his silence was do-nothingness. They were wrong. And Belsher was the one who waited until Paterson retired before tossing his hat into the ring.

Al MacMillan was Paterson's Ottawa legislative assistant. He remained on the Hill for many years, later moving into the civil service after Paterson retired. Then, in the nineties, he sensed a call into ministry and planted Bridlewood church. It is now a congregation of 300 and one of a cluster of rapidly growing evangelical churches in Kanata that are responding with vigour to the spiritual and creative needs of an innovative high-tech community. Some Ottawa-area Christian leaders say that providing spiritual leadership to that kind of community is like herding cats. The biblical analogies about shepherds and sheep require a little reinterpretation.

More Faithful than We Think

The MacMillans are more typical of Christian servant leadership than one might think. Many Christian support staff on the Hill have worked for politicians in different parties through the years. They know that the presence of God can penetrate any party apparatus. Sometimes, a sense of biblically based servant leadership has, in fact, brought reconciliation despite the efforts of those who see adversarialism as king.

Goldie stayed on the Hill. She is personal assistant to Environment Minister David Anderson. In case no one noticed, he is a Liberal. She is only one of many Christian support staffers working for Liberal politicians. They are there for a reason, and it might even have something to do with the grace of God.

Goldie retired from the Hill in 2003, shortly before Anderson left the federal cabinet.

The part of Al MacMillan's sermon during Colleen's funeral that really blew my mind was his quoting of Rudyard Kipling. He worked it into a cluster of biblical passages about hope, promise and resurrection. The particular Kipling poem to which I refer is well-remembered from grade 10 English literature, taken more years ago than I care to remember.

Part of it goes like this:

> When earth's last picture is painted
> And the tubes are twisted and dried
> And the oldest colours have faded
> And the youngest critic has died.
>
> We shall rest, and faith we shall need it
> Lie down for an aeon or two.

'Til the Master of all good workmen
Shall set us to work anew.

*I don't know much about Sir Rudyard's theological
vicissitudes, but I remembered that poem because, to me at
least, it breathed the spirit of God. As I pondered the words,
I think I understood a little more of the sense of hope that
emanates from evangelical funerals. For it is the fact that,
even long after we rest a while beyond the grave, God will
have for the Christian many things to do that will make a difference wherever he places us.*

Evangelical funerals aside, the political activity of
evangelical, reformed and charismatic Christians, for the
most part, has integrated quite effectively for at least the
past twenty-five years. That is the period of time that the
Evangelical Fellowship of Canada has virtually been an
equal partner in Christian influence with the Canadian
Council of Churches and the Canadian Conference of
Catholic Bishops.

In the next chapter, we will look at a story involving a
group that has not mainstreamed in the Canadian political
process quite as much as other denominations. The reasons, sociological and historic, are worth noting.

Chapter Twelve

Anatomy of a Parental Rights Controversy

In "doing politics christianly..." #33, written July 28, 2001, I picked up on the issue of the parental right to discipline, as it had been publicized in the conflict between social workers and a southwestern Ontario church. The approach taken, in this case, was to try to accurately identify the varying spiritual and cultural influences in the church in question.

WHICH CHURCH OF GOD?

The headspace of this particular writer, you need to understand, includes a section for denominational trivia. At least, "trivia" is the way some of my friends would describe it. But I believe that one often needs to recognize the trivia to understand the issues.

The now-famous but still anonymous seven children seized screaming and kicking from their parents in the quiet southwestern Ontario town of Aylmer were from a Church of God congregation. Given my penchant for "trivia pursuit," the first question was: "Which Church of God?"

As it turns out, the question actually has some validity.

Consider some of the wording of Ontario Court Justice Michael O'Dea's order, returning the children to their parents. True, he said that the parents were to refrain from spanking until family court could deal with the case on September 6 [2001]. But there was a further directive to the Family and Children's Services (FCS) of St. Thomas and Elgin: FCS must continue to learn about the religious traditions and cultural background of the family.

That last item should involve at least some research into which particular kind of Church of God this group is and is not.

I wondered, at first, if it was part of any one of the following groups.

- *Church of God in Christ (Mennonite), also known as Holdeman. Characteristics of this group include refraining from the use of radio and television. Their men wear beards, and white prayer caps adorn the heads of their women. They follow many of the traditional Mennonite teachings, including that of pacifism.*
- *The "Needed Truth" Brethren, a conservative manifestation of the Christian Brethren (often nicknamed Plymouth Brethren). They identify their churches in particular cities as the "Church of God in (name of city)."*
- *The Worldwide Church of God, the group that gained considerable attention a few years ago through the leadership of the late Herbert W. Armstrong and his son, Garner Ted Armstrong. In more recent years, this group, which had communicated mainly through television, radio and magazine media, has settled more into the development of local churches. In so doing, except for its Saturday*

worship practice, it has moved into mainstream Christian evangelicalism.

- *The Philadelphia Church of God, a spinoff of some of Worldwide's more recent reorganizations.*
- *Church of God (Anderson), a group that is part of the Holiness movement whose other denominations include the Salvation Army, the Free Methodists, the Wesleyans and parts of the Evangelical Missionary Church. The Anderson part of the name relates to the fact that its roots are in Anderson, Indiana.*
- *Church of God (Cleveland, Tennessee), cousins within the Holiness movement to the Anderson group, differing in minor ways and drawing from dissimilar sociological strata.*

As it turns out, the Anderson group is closest to the mark. The Church of God in Aylmer is a part of a 1910 split from the Church of God (Anderson). Its people sometimes refer to themselves as the "restoration group" because they restored some of the earlier and, perhaps, more rigid practices that the Andersoners had abandoned. They have churches scattered throughout the United States and Canada.

The suggestion that they are a Mennonite group comes from the fact that they have attracted a fair number of Mennonites into their church, including some recent immigrants from Mennonite colonies in Mexico. To that extent, they are not unlike many evangelical denominations that attracted numerous Mennonites into their churches in areas where Mennonite settlement was heavy. In more recent years, the trend has gone the other way, as well. Some Mennonite congregations — Willingdon and Northview in British Columbia and Meeting Place in

Winnipeg — are among Canada's largest evangelical churches. And those churches include many non-Mennonite names on their rolls.

When the Family and Children's Service people do what Justice O'Dea wants them to, there are several things they will want to try to understand that relate both to style and substance.

One of the key figures in the Aylmer controversy is Henry Hildebrandt, the pastor of the Aylmer Church of God. In dress and appearance, he looks like the leader of a conservative type of Mennonite church. When he opens his mouth, however, he is pure Southern preacher. Close your eyes and you might think you are listening to E.V. Hill or T.D. Jakes, the two black preachers who have found the most acceptance in non-black evangelical circles in North America.

It would appear from the television coverage that the music draws strongly from Southern gospel — both white and black variety. It has a joyful tone with strong harmony and gives no hint of the sort of stern outlook that insists that the discipline of children is useless if it does not hurt a bit.

These are matters of style. But Hildebrandt has been enunciating the substance of the church's teaching about the use of the "rod."

Several organizations have been supporting the church's view in response to what they see as the "liberal fundamentalism" of social service bureaucrats — the people who want to ban spanking without taking into account the religious or cultural context in which it is practised.

Home-schooling organizations are particularly concerned, because they involve people who, by virtue of their family structures, are both the parents and the teachers of their own children.

One of the long-standing issues surrounding a biblical approach to discipline is its impact on the children who receive it.

As a preteen, I was exposed to the Bible conferences that formed a significant part of the Christian Brethren culture. Every Thanksgiving and Easter, hundreds of Victoria Brethren assembly members gathered for holiday weekend preaching sessions followed by sumptuous meals. At one of those conferences, the speaker was Donald McIntosh, a missionary to the Dominican Republic, who was known for his then radical contemporary interpretations of controversial passages of Scripture.

On this particular occasion, he was holding forth on the text in Ephesians 6 that speaks of the need for children to obey their parents. Of course, all the parents were eyeing their own broods, dressed in Sunday best, to ensure that they were listening carefully.

Suddenly, McIntosh shifted gears and moved into the second part of that particular passage, in which parents are admonished – and here I am quoting from the Living Bible – "Don't keep on scolding and nagging your children, making them angry and resentful. Rather, bring them up with the loving discipline the Lord himself approves, with suggestions and godly advice."

Now, there were a number of the church leaders who were not too happy with McIntosh expounding on that passage in a group where there were both parents and children present. I know for a fact that some of those leaders had a few strokes of verbal discipline for their wayward guest preacher. Indeed, there were at least a few children present who, as I recall, were known to be resentful and angry with the kind of treatment they received from their parents. But the elders opined that the kids were resentful because they were brats whose wills needed to be broken. Who was right? In retrospect, who knows?

Perhaps some of the anti-spanking movement feeds on resentment built on misunderstood relationships developed in particularly doctrinaire homes. But Justice O'Dea has done well to include in his judgment the admonition to the FCS to ensure that they understand the religious traditions and cultural background of the family.

The shift from Hill politics to denominational trivia for this particular edition of "doing politics christianly..." will hopefully shed a bit of light on the way some Christians do "family" politics. The spanking question fits within the cluster of life and family issues that captures the attention of a fair number of federal politicians. For that reason, it will be always with us.

In the next chapter, we will take a look at David Smith, recently-minted senator, key Chrétien strategist and the man who claims to have gotten God into the preamble of the Canadian constitution.

Chapter Thirteen

Faith's Role in Political Party Strategy

This chapter is about David Smith, Trudeau cabinet member, Pentecostal ministers' son and brother, key Liberal strategist and, now, senator.

Smith also might be described as the Liberal secret weapon. He is a Baptist who keeps the faith, and so is his wife, Heather. He mixes with the most sophisticated of Canadian political society with ease and skill. Also, as much as that, he listens with care to his two brothers who are Pentecostal ministers, and he has deep roots in evangelical Christianity.

His late father, C.B. Smith, held key Pentecostal pastorates in, among other places, two capital cities, Ottawa and Victoria. One brother, Robert, is long-time pastor of the 2,500-strong London Gospel Temple. Another, George, has pastored large churches in Vancouver and Edmonton and, about ten years ago, became president of Missions of Mercy, a Pentecostal relief and development agency working in Calcutta. Its founder, the late Mark Buntain, is known as the "Pentecostal Mother Teresa."

All of this is to say that while David and Heather Smith keep their church home at Toronto's imposing

Yorkminster Park Baptist, they effectively network the broader evangelical community.

Before being appointed to the Senate, Smith earned his daily bread as chair of Fraser Milner Casgrain (now known as Fraser Finerty), one of Canada's largest law firms. In his spare time, he was a key Liberal strategist for Ontario and, later, co-chair of the Liberal campaign for the 2000 election.

As a low-profile, high-energy type of evangelical, he spent a fair amount of intellect looking for federal candidates, especially in Ontario. He wanted people who could please that ten to fifteen percent of the population who take their Christian faith seriously enough that they would vote for a person who understands their concerns.

Not that the law firm he headed always necessarily looked to the Liberals for their national salvation. Smith acknowledged that, when the Calgary firm of Casgrain merged into Fraser Milner, it brought a fair number of Alliance/Reform lawyer support to the table, not the least of whom was Andrea Manning Kroon, daughter of Preston and Sandra.

And which law firm was the largest corporate contributor to Alliance coffers in 2000? Why, FMC, of course, according to the *HillTimes*, the Parliament Hill tabloid. The figure was in the neighbourhood of $120,000 — apparently a write-off for some work done by the firm for the Alliance.

One thing a Christian journalist discovers when he moves from west to east, as I did six years ago, is that the massive evangelical support for the Alliance in the west did not transfer into Ontario. There are several explanations, the most logical of which had to do with Conservative/Alliance vote-splitting and the fact that so many people who might otherwise support a united small-c conservative effort park their votes with the Liberals. (The 2004 federal election results in Ontario, while not giving the new Conservative party the sweep it hoped for, did stop the vote-splitting in a couple of dozen ridings.)

The other logical reason is that people like Smith know how to place the right Liberals in the right places at the right time.

The following "Capital Views" piece I did for *ChristianCurrent* in August 2002, when Smith was appointed to the Senate, offers some clues as to the way in which both David and Heather operate in the legal/political role. At the end of it, I will comment particularly on Heather's role in the unfolding of the same-sex marriage debate.

How God Slipped into the Charter of Rights

Newly-minted Senator David Smith speaks with modest pride about the role he played in getting God mentioned in the Canadian Charter of Rights and Freedom.

Smith was a junior minister in Pierre Trudeau's cabinet in 1981. Trudeau was experiencing some angst over whether to recognize God in the Charter.

Knowing that Smith was related to – and respectful of – several Pentecostal ministers, Trudeau sought his advice.

Smith communicated the PM's anxiety to family friend Brian Stiller, another Pentecostal minister who was just beginning to make his mark as leader of the Evangelical Fellowship of Canada. They checked out which Canadian seminaries were producing the most new ministers. Not surprisingly, the winners were the evangelical schools, many in western Canada, where Liberal voters are often as scarce as hen's teeth.

As the tale goes, they prepared a set of charts to back up Smith's presentation to Trudeau. The PM would be wise, he suggested, to use the God *word.*

Thus, today, the Charter begins with the words: "Whereas Canada is founded upon principles that recognize the supremacy of God and the rule of law...."

Fast forward to the second week of July 2002.

Smith, who is widely viewed as a key strategist in the Liberals' remarkable electoral success since 1993, had just been appointed to the Senate. A few days later, the Ontario Superior Court ruled that the federal prohibition against legally sanctioned gay and lesbian unions is discriminatory and unconstitutional. Then it suspended implementation of its judgment for two years.

One of the three judges ruling in the case is Heather Smith. Now, Justice Smith is known as a good judge in her own right, no matter what prime minister appointed her and to whom she is married. But the suspension of implementation is both a gift and a challenge for the reigning Liberals. Undoubtedly, the feds will use the time to appeal the decision to the Supreme Court of Canada.

In fact, there are several options open to the government. One is to accept the proposal of several religious groups from across the theological spectrum – the concept of domestic registered partnerships free of conjugal implications.

Under such a registration scheme, the state can ensure that no particular group is endowed with, or deprived of, particular rights. The various faiths that have a stake in the "rites" connection – the social and spiritual side of marriage – can act without state hindrance.

Ironically, a church helped spearhead the Ontario same-sex marriage case – Toronto's gay-oriented Metropolitan

Community Church. In most respects, MCC's pastor Brent Hawkes sounds like an evangelical minister. Admittedly, the exception, the MCC's sanctioning of same-sex unions, is big enough to drive a cruise ship through.

The federal Liberals hold all the cards on this issue, no matter who is prime minister in two years. The opposition will have its challenges. It could create leadership issues in both the Tory and NDP parties – and perhaps even the Bloc. For the Alliance, the challenge will be to behave like a real, and credible, official opposition.

During Paul Martin's deficit slashing exercise, the CA's predecessor, the Reform party, was often credited with forcing him toward fiscal conservatism. Among the results of this are increased economic efficiency and recovery. If the Alliance can keep the heat on the Liberals about positive traditional family values, the social effects could be equally salutary.

In commenting on the role of Justice Heather Smith in all this, let's begin with the influence of the Reform party. One of its most intriguing accomplishments, apart from forcing Martin to eliminate the deficit and reduce the debt, occurred on June 8, 1999. That day, the House of Commons passed a Reform motion to codify the definition of marriage as being between a man and a woman. Only fifty-five in the House were against the motion, and most of the Liberals, including the present prime minister and several cabinet ministers, were among the 216 who voted for it.

So, when the Ontario Superior Court gave the Liberals a two-year reprieve on legalizing same-sex unions, the general view in the House was that there was a little time to sort this out. However, the Ontario Court of Appeal (in a separate dossier) ruled that the man–woman definition of marriage was unconstitutional—as did the counterpart courts in British Columbia and Quebec.

Instead of appealing those decisions to the Supreme Court of Canada, the government (to the delight of the gay activist lobby) decided to try cobbling together legislation that would meet the courts' constitutional objections.

In the summer and fall of 2003, the gay marriage debate was in full swing. Baptist Heather Smith had put the cat among the pigeons, who, of course, will come to roost, in the next election if not before.

In order to understand the role of the Christian faith in this debate, it is good to try to clarify the rules, the players and the goalposts, any of which can change in fifteen minutes.

In an analysis piece headlined "Politicians Playing with Fire" appearing on page A-18 in the *National Post* on August 2, 2003, University of Toronto historian Michael Bliss made this observation:

> Sensitive politicians in all countries traditionally try to handle explosive social issues involving race and religion with kid gloves. Don't pit ethnic groups against one another; don't split society on religious lines or on fundamental moral issues. Search for compromises; prevaricate; be courageously cowardly if necessary. Politicians simply cannot offer easy leadership on divisive social issues, but rather have to follow the tide of opinion, brokering competing positions and waiting for common denominators to develop. Certain problems involving conflicting claims to rights and privileges within society really ought to be left to the courts to sort

out. I think the difficult question of the definition of marriage is one such problem.

When modernization and social liberalism first came to Quebec in the 1960s, all of the progressive people in Canada thought the Jean Lesage government was immensely popular for its education, anti-clerical and other reforms. It was a huge surprise when the Lesage Liberals were turfed out of office in the 1966 provincial election because of the backlash against the rapid pace of social change. At heart, at least for a while, Quebecers were more conservative than all but the religious elites realized.

Now evangelicals generally support the separation of church and state, and so do Catholics, except in jurisdictions where they dominate. But the moderates of both religions — the former of which is decentralized to local congregations in its form of government, and the latter much more hierarchical — would agree on the following: devout politicians, judges or bureaucrats may, and should, let their faith inform and shape their circle of influence in the political process.

Out at the fringes of faith influence, the most charismatic or conservative theocrats would argue that, for God to properly run the country, the Christians should be in charge of the levers of power. If push comes to shove, they would agree with the premise on which Islamic fundamentalism operates.

Thus, it was interesting to watch the various clusters and coalitions shape up once Justice Minister Martin Cauchon sent the government's proposed same-sex legislation to the Supreme Court of Canada for review before unleashing it on the House of Commons.

First out of the starting gate was an interfaith coalition consisting of, among others, evangelicals, Catholics and Muslims. They wanted to retain the man–woman definition of marriage but would not be opposed to some sort of legal recognition of same-sex unions.

A day or two later, a pro-family group, organized by Canada Family Action Coalition, Focus on the Family and REAL Women, weighed in. They did not want to be associated with any such formal recognition — even if it did not use the "m" word. Not long after, a group of liberal Christians and Jews noted they were not opposed to same-sex marriage.

Then came the juggernaut: the Vatican. It stood firmly against both the change in definition and legal recognition of same-sex unions. This was to be expected. Catholic officialdom invariably ties together abortion and contraception almost seamlessly because of the insistence that, in the mind of God, there is an unbreakable philosophical linkage. Pro-life evangelicals, however, have not codified any such stances on contraception. So when evangelical and Catholic pro-lifers work together, they mutually recognize it is their common ground that is to be accentuated, not their differences.

On the same-sex marriage issue, evangelicals and Catholics will find common cause in the areas where they agree, finding unity against a common foe to be more productive than tangling over exactly where to draw the lines of battle.

Now the Vatican has all the resources of the Magisterium at its disposal: Vatican law, the Scriptures, apostolic authority and the sway of many papal encyclicals. The Vatican also expected the Canadian bishops to fall in line. Some did. Bishop Fred Henry of Calgary more or less consigned devout Catholic Jean Chrétien to eternal damnation if he okayed same-sex marriage.

As a body, the Canadian Conference of Catholic Bishops was a little more diplomatic. After all, it had already approved the concept of registered domestic partnerships — the legalizing of various kinds of permanent unions but without the conjugal implications (in plainer language: acceptance of the Pierre Trudeau dictum that the state has no place in the bedrooms of the nation). While the Vatican was asking that the bishops order the priests to preach against same-sex marriage in their August 3, 2003, homilies, Canadian Catholic leaders cut their pastors varying amounts of slack. Cardinal Aloysius Ambrozic backed the Vatican order while his Montreal counterpart, Cardinal Jean-Claude Turcotte, declined to issue the directive.

Gay activists and fellow travellers, meanwhile, lined up on the side favouring full-blown same-sex marriage; groups ranged from a coalition of liberal Christians and Jews to the pro-gay Metropolitan Community Church and EGALE (Equality for Gays and Lesbians). There was also one radical spinoff, whose ideas are shaped by Judith Levine, sociologist author of *Harmful to Minors: The Perils of Protecting Children from Sex*. She wrote in the *Village Voice*, July 23–29, that gay marriage was not enough. There needed to be legalization for multi-partner marriages, with no limitation on age, gender or number of partners. Levine is not exactly your mainstream gay activist, and many of them find her an embarrassment. Also, she does not carry nearly the weight that her Catholic counterparts would on the other side.

We started off this chapter with the David and Heather Smith story and moved through the shaping of the same-sex marriage debate that his political party and her court's ruling helped to ignite. At the time this book appears in print, we will be closer to knowing for sure exactly how the debate turned out.

I leave this one thought, drawn from some comments I made shortly after the November 2000 election, when the Canadian Alliance failed to make a breakthrough in Ontario, the Liberals returned with a third majority under Jean Chrétien and, to rub salt in the CA wounds, virtually swept Ontario.

Some of my Christian friends in the CA, in their grief, wondered why the spiritually bankrupt Liberals were re-elected. My response, recalling the Old Testament anger of Elijah (1 Kings 19) toward God for not sending the enemy packing, was that "perhaps there are still enough people in the Liberal party who have not yet bowed the knee to Baal, to spare them from the judgment of God."

There is a touch of irony in that statement because the fact is, God can do his work through serious and intelligent Christians in any political party. That is why I tend to encourage people to think in terms of doing politics Christianly, so that, no matter what the circumstances, the actions and witness of Christians will be present. That makes more sense, in this corner, than assuming that God has appointed a particular party or leader to bring the nation out of the political and spiritual wilderness and into the promised land and, ultimately, the new Jerusalem.

Thus, the interesting roles of David and Heather Smith.

Chapter Fourteen

Jake Epp and Matthew Coon Come

In this chapter, we will look at two politicians, one from the Mulroney era and the other from the world of First Nations politics: Jake Epp and Matthew Coon Come.

This next piece, written August 18, 2001, sketches out a brief history of Jake Epp, who held the Indian affairs portfolio in the short-lived Joe Clark government and health and energy posts in Brian Mulroney's cabinet.

Watch for a reference to a "faith-based" funding initiative that well pre-dated anything George W. Bush did south of the border.

JAKE EPP: LEADER OR FACILITATOR?

Periodically, Jake Epp's distinguished white-haired image flashes onto the evangelical political radar screen. At sixty-one, he is seen as a bridge between the past and present, the Alliance and the Conservatives, the evangelical world and the rest of the body politic. This week, he was briefly touted as a potential Alliance leadership candidate. He all but closed the door on that possibility.

I first covered Epp in 1988, when he was the Tory

health minister. Editing a now-deceased Christian newspaper in Toronto, I received a tip from his office suggesting his day-care proposals might be interesting for a Christian audience. Sure enough, a few choice paragraphs were buried in the proposals. They revealed the possibility that a church or a group of church families might be able to obtain capital funding from the feds to add to their church building, conditional on a daycare centre operating long term in that building.

The proposal was a new step: not just operating assistance but a capital loan or grant. Its significance to Christians was the recognition — long before George Bush's faith-based initiatives were moot south of the border — that church groups were potentially compatible agents of social service.

For Jake Epp, at the time the top evangelical Christian in the federal cabinet, the proposal was a subtle signal that churches and Christian groups had a valid place in the delivery of daycare. In a sense, Epp was standing in the gap between two adversaries — those Christians who believe that stay-at-home moms are the only people who should provide daycare and those on the other side who believe that it is the state's responsibility.

Epp's point, if I understood him correctly, was that groups of Christian parents holding similar child-rearing views could band together to support each other in child care. As well, they could reach out to their communities in Christ's name to fulfil an unmet need.

Eventually the daycare proposal died a natural death, as do many of the plans of governments of various stripes. But Epp's particular gap-standing approach showed itself again when he was working within the Brian Mulroney cabinet to spearhead what was described as "consensus" legislation to regulate abortion.

The reaction to the legislation proved stressful to Epp. The abortion-on-demand people dumped on him from great heights for trying to draw trimester timelines on abortion's legality. More ironically, however, many of his fellow evangelical believers crucified him for not pushing for an outright ban.

At the time, Reform was just beginning its rise. Some of the Christians who had been Epp's supporters threw in with Reform and, in fact, undermined the regard with which he had been held in the Manitoba Bible belt riding he had served so well for many years.

For Epp, the upshot was that his prime minister released him from the abortion cauldron by moving him into the energy portfolio, which he served with distinction until he left politics a few years later.

The abortion issue was catalytic to the creation of great animosity between the Mulroney "God squad" MPs, who disappeared with their party after the 1993 election, and their Reform replacements, many of whom were also evangelical Christians. Epp was one of those who viewed Reform with some seemingly justifiable bitterness.

In late 1998, the Canadian Alliance was beginning to stir in the United Alternative womb. Epp was turning up at UA exploratory meetings. I called to ask him about it. The result was a story I wrote for Report Magazine, *outlining the former health minister's belief that it was time for reconciliation. He was quoted urging Christians in both the Conservative and Reform parties to act on their conciliatory instincts. He also confessed to his own past bitterness, saying that it was time to put it behind him.*

Subsequently, Epp joined the Canadian Alliance and threw his support behind Stockwell Day. In so doing, though, he allowed that Preston Manning had been a good leader.

Manning's main flaw, Epp suggested, was his unwillingness to deal directly with conflict within the party, handing that responsibility instead off to lieutenants.

Then, this past week [August 2001], Epp's name emerged as a possible leadership candidate. It was a logical suggestion in the light of a clear sense among many on the political right that the Tories and Alliance need ultimately to come together either as a coalition or a merger.

Yet, Epp's approach seems to be, as it has been for the past three years, that he would like to use his skills as a facilitator rather than tackle a leadership role. If he was to become leader, he would see it as an interim role that would serve the longer term facilitation process. He is, after all, sixty-one and recently retired from the executive vice-presidency of Trans Canada Pipelines, where he went after leaving politics. It seems, these days, that sixty-plus is over the hill.

My guess is that Epp will wait awhile, to see if the Alliance leadership race turns out to be a combined Alliance–Tory contest. He is probably one of the very few people in Canada who could broker a principled consensus that would satisfy most elements of both parties.

For Jake Epp, much did not turn out as he might have hoped. His offer to be a facilitator, if it was taken up, was practised without fanfare. He was not among the "emissaries" who advised Stephen Harper and Peter MacKay on the CA/PC merger.

Any Christian politician in his or her forties or fifties would do well to look back to Epp's heyday when, at their age, he advanced some fairly bold, if not completely successful, initiatives. They grew, in part at least, out of his Christian faith.

As for Matthew Coon Come, we will look at two pieces. The first is "doing politics christianly..." #32, written on July 21, 2001, which talks about the election of this new grand chief, who was unabashedly an evangelical Christian.

FOR WHOM DOES THE CHRISTIAN LEADER SPEAK?

Much has been made of the Christian commitment – Pentecostal variety – of Matthew Coon Come, chief of the Assembly of First Nations.

I can't help but notice, however, that many people are reacting to a number of his public pronouncements, commending him at times and otherwise wondering about some of his seeming contradictions. Those pronouncements provide the basis for an interesting case study for those who want to try to answer the question: "For whom does the Christian leader speak?"

As far as I am aware, Chief Coon Come has been completely unavailable for interviews with non-First Nations Christian journalists. His Christian stance was covered soon after his election, with a spate of stories about:

- *His conversion to Christ through the influence of an American evangelist*
- *His willingness to let the "baggage" of his "white man's religion" show itself, at whatever the cost, in his run for the First Nations top job*
- *The work that he did in the field of relationship building and healing, while a member of Woodvale Pentecostal Church in the Ottawa suburb of Nepean*

There have been two further opportunities to interpret his views and actions from a Christian viewpoint. One came with his widely-quoted suggestion that First Nations leaders smoke and drink too much and are, for that reason, sometimes unsuitable role models for younger people.

The second was when he was seen, without fanfare, attending a Transformations II *conference in Ottawa. The conference was one of several held across Canada to launch the release of the* Transformations II *video and was attended by about 1,000 people.*

Transformations *has received a fair amount of play in Christian media in Canada. In brief, the videos are produced by researcher George Otis Jr. and are intended for the purpose of exploring a number of the remarkable examples of Christian renewal occurring in various nations and cultures throughout the world.*

One of the renewals featured in Transformations II *has happened in the past few years in several Inuit villages in northern Quebec and adjacent islands. It has been sweeping through both Anglican and Pentecostal churches in these villages and has included such phenomena as "rushing mighty winds."*

More to the point, regarding community transformation, the suicide rate has reportedly dropped markedly in these villages, as spiritual renewal has replaced despair for many of these young people.

The First Nations chief indicated to some of his fellow attendees at the Ottawa conference that he was particularly interested in the Quebec reports and wanted to use the information from the videos to advance his understanding of the subject.

With respect to Chief Coon Come's comments about smoking and drinking, it should be noted that during last week's AFN conference in Halifax he apologized for them, indicating that he felt the kind of publicity they had received was hurtful to the First Nations' cause. However, the comments originated from the pietistic underpinnings of the evangelical faith that is so much a part of his life. The pinpointing of the damage caused by the use – or at the very least, the misuse – of alcohol and tobacco is very much an essence of the doctrines surrounding personal holiness. Pentecostals in both Caucasian and native communities would more or less be in agreement on that basic message.

Yet, an apology from the chief may have been a necessity. That is because he is the leader of a pluralistic and eclectic body, whose main commonality is the aboriginal makeup of its membership. Particularly, some of the practices related to native spirituality might run afoul of evangelical taboos. As a First Nations leader, however, Chief Coon Come cannot attack them with impunity.

Two recent Coon Come communiqués provide some additional insights into the kinds of leadership pressures he faces. About two months ago, a strongly-worded statement virtually ruled out any dialogue with Canadian Alliance aboriginal critics. The statement was seen by many in the non-native community to be a pre-emptive strike. Its unstated point was that just because he and the leader of Her Majesty's Loyal Opposition (Stockwell Day) were evangelical Christians did not mean they could speak the same language on such issues.

One of the Canadian Alliance proposals had been to share ideas on private and common property ownership. There have been a number of indicators from AFN leaders that such discussions are outside the purview of their governance methods and culture.

Then, during the Halifax conference, the chief took a

similar hard line against the Indian Act overhaul proposal coming from Richard Nault, the Indian affairs minister.

Both responses were indicative of the strong stances that helped him win the election over former AFN chief Phil Fontaine, who was seen as having been too conciliatory toward non-native political leaders.

All of the above is stated within the context of occasional e-mails I receive from Bill Chu, an old friend from Vancouver who heads up an advocacy organization known as Chinese Christians in Action (CCIA).

CCIA is active in encouraging reconciliation between native and non-native communities through an application of the conciliatory and restorative justice aspects of the gospel.

Chu makes the point with me that I need to be more critical of things such as market economics and compassionate conservatism if I am to act prophetically to help right the wrongs of history against our First Nations people.

I take his point without rancour. CCIA may well be in a better position to build bridges toward First Nations people, whose cultures have created a different set of values with respect to property and governance, than others whose experience is quite different.

The second piece on Coon Come was written for *ChristianCurrent* in July 2003, shortly after he was defeated in his run for a second term as grand chief of the Assembly of First Nations.

It grew out of word that came two-thirds of the way through his term as grand chief that he was involved, in his spare time, in an interesting church-planting project in Ottawa.

A Turn in the Road for the Coon Comes

Matthew Coon Come handily defeated Phil Fontaine three years ago, when he ran to replace him as Chief of the Assembly of First Nations (AFN). Last month, however, the tables were turned. Chief Coon Come ran third in a field of three as Chief Fontaine was handily returned to the Canada's aboriginal "premiership."

Commenting on his defeat, Coon Come remarked cryptically that he had received the support he deserved.

Indeed, from a Christian viewpoint, his AFN watch has produced its share of conundrums. Soon after his election, Coon Come's strong evangelical Christian faith was the subject of a couple of columns in the National Post. *He made the point in one of those columns that he was prepared to risk rejection for taking on a "white man's religion."*

Apart from that NP *exposure, he proved reluctant to talk, for either the secular or Christian media, about his Christian faith. Yet, he and his wife, MaryAnn, were involved during his tenure in several aspects of charismatic Christian activity, both in Ottawa and in events that took place in other parts of Canada. Last fall,* ChristianCurrent's *Ottawa edition ran an advertisement for a new Ottawa church, Harvest Glory, which included the information that Matthew and MaryAnn were the associate pastors.*

It was already well known throughout the evangelical community in the capital that the Coon Comes had been members of Woodvale Church, a large west-side Pentecostal congregation, before they had moved to the Montreal area so he could head up the Cree nation in Quebec.

Thus, his role in Harvest Glory proved to be an attention-getter. To get more on the story, I attended a Sunday evening service at which the Coon Comes were active participants.

MaryAnn was the more vocal of the two in the free-form service attended by about forty people, drawn from at least half a dozen ethnic streams. She exhibited clear gifts in the areas of prayer and what charismatic Christians often describe as "prophecy."

Matthew, explaining later that he saw his role as expressing the "gift of helps," was kept busy providing backup guitar to the pastor's husband, who keyboarded for the worship team. Further, he offered quiet words of encouragement to worshippers who were seeking individual counsel and helped "catch" some who fell back in a worship experience sometimes described as "being slain in the Spirit."

A few days later, he spoke to an outreach breakfast designed to communicate the basic Christian faith to friends of church members who had not yet committed their lives to Christ.

I was impressed by the humility of both the Coon Comes and by the obviously mature and intelligent relationship they had with their teenage children and other friends who attended the service with them. In that context, it was hard to envisage this man as the seemingly combative head of a community of 500,000 people stretched across Canada. The fact is, though, that charismatic Christianity has extensive influence in many of Canada's First Nations in Anglican, Pentecostal and independent churches. So, in that sense, many aboriginals have adopted this "white man's religion." And the Coon Comes have aided that trend.

In due course, political scientists may offer some interpretation for the former chief's statement in defeat about getting the support he deserved.

But don't be surprised if the Coon Comes become more involved in Christian ministry. They take counsel from time to time from Ottawa-based Pentecostal evangelist Bill Prankard, who has both a widespread television ministry and a strong outreach across northern Canada. Further, they have kept close contact with another Christian Cree leader, Kenny Blacksmith, who spearheads the Gathering of All Nations events that bring hundreds of Christians together for worship and renewal in both the capital and at a First Nations retreat site in northern Quebec.

Watch for the Coon Comes to turn Matthew's political defeat into new and previously unavailable opportunities for communicating their faith in the aboriginal "public square." Jake Epp has proven that there is life after politics, as has his sometime Christian rival, Preston Manning. Now, it is Matthew Coon Come's turn.

Chapter Fifteen

Out of Service Comes Honour

In chapter nine, I wrote briefly of Gerald Vandezande, the founder of Citizens for Public Justice, and told his story within the context of his being made a member of the Order of Canada. Eyeing these honours, I cannot help but notice that a fair number of known Christians make the lists.

Many of them are what we might call "professionals," such as priests or other Christian ministers who, in the course of their vocation, contribute greatly to the larger society. In a journalist's lexicon, they could be referred to as the "dog bites man" kind of story. Out of Christian commitment and vocation comes a penchant to serve society in the name of Jesus. And out of that service comes an honour bestowed by the citizenry of the nation.

There were a few evangelicals and near-evangelicals in the lists of the 4,000-plus who have been named to one level or another of the Order of Canada whose primary vocation was unrelated or only partly connected to the professional Christian ministry in its narrowest sense. In these next few paragraphs, taken from "doing politics christianly…" #37, #38 and #39, you will meet a few of these people and perhaps learn some surprising things about them.

Lloyd Mackey

CALLS TO ORDER

The periodic Order of Canada appointment announce-ments often represent an effective antidote to the argument that the Christian faith, particularly in its evangelical form, has been marginalized in Canadian society.

This week, there were several appointments to the Order that caught the interest of this particular watchful eye. They are Gerald Vandezande, Henry Friesen, Ray Speaker and Murray McCheyne Thomson.

As indicated above, Vandezande's citation appears earlier in this book, in a different exploratory context.

Each of these people is a Christian whose faith perspec-tive falls in or near the evangelical part of the spectrum. Only one, Vandezande, has worked in a vocation where his Christian faith was an integral part of the job description. Thomson came close, as I will note later. Friesen and Speaker are both serious believers whose faith and Christian networks have had a lot to do with their work and accomplishments.

Friesen was promoted within the order to become a companion, the highest designation. Thomson was made an officer, the middle designation. They join a list of about 4,000 Canadians who have been honoured since 1967 in twice-annual ceremonies at Rideau Hall in Ottawa. The ceremony, the particular designation, plus the wording of the citation that describes the reason for the honour are all the end result of a complex nomination and decision-making process.

Today, we will look at three of the above-mentioned cur-rent honourees. Next week, I will speak of five others who have made the lists in the past: Ben Heppner, Robert Thompson, Cathy Nicoll, Henry Hildebrand and Clark Bentall.

More Faithful than We Think

Murray McCheyne Thomson is a member of the Society of Friends (Quakers). His father was a Presbyterian, and later United, minister, and his parents spent time as missionaries in China. That "McCheyne" in his name is a hint of the regard in which his parents held the famous Presbyterian preacher, Robert Murray McCheyne.

He is a co-founder of Project Ploughshares, an organization that has drawn much of its support from the traditional peace churches, Mennonite and Friends (Quakers). He has played the same role for Peace Brigades International and Peacefund Canada. The practical side of his work is synthesized in his Order of Canada citation: "Over many years, both the federal government and the United Nations have called on his expertise as an advisor on disarmament and arms control."

Henry Friesen is not so obvious about his faith, but neither does he hide it. An endocrinologist by profession, he headed the former Medical Research Council of Canada for many years. His Ottawa time gave him the opportunity to become a well-respected member of Cedarview Alliance Church. Now, from Winnipeg, where he is able to tie in with the University of Manitoba where he taught for many years, he serves as board chair of Genome Canada.

Ray Speaker is another whose faith speaks quietly. He served in the Alberta Social Credit cabinet of Ernest Manning, continued in a similar role in the Conservative governments of Peter Lougheed and Don Getty, then became part of the federal Reform party's "class of '93." He comes from Enchant, a place where a number of Scandinavian immigrants formed an Evangelical Free Church, the first such in Canada, around the turn of the twentieth century. That particular denomination went on to spearhead the development of Trinity Western University.

Lloyd Mackey

Speaker is thus continuity personified. He is out of the limelight now but is still viewed by many Christian and conservative leaders as some of the glue that helped hold together faith and philosophical interest that otherwise would have flown asunder.

AND THESE HAVE GONE BEFORE

Commenting last week on the most recent Order of Canada recipients, I made mention of five who had gone before who could be safely identified as evangelical Christians. In checking their citations, I had a test question: "Is there anything in what was said officially about their honour that identifies by either word or action that their Christian faith was a factor in the way they lived their lives?"

All five came back positively, but each in a different way. In some cases, the point of witness was the nature of the honouree's vocation; in others, a personal characteristic; and in others still, an institution with which they identified. In several cases, there was more than one witness point.

Of the five, Ben Heppner and Henry Hildebrand are still alive. Heppner is at the peak of his career. Hildebrand has long since officially retired but keeps in close touch with the institution with which he was associated. Clark Bentall and Robert Thompson died in the late nineties. They are only five of the 4,000 plus Canadians who have been made members, officers or companions of the Order of Canada since it was set up at the time of our nation's centennial in 1967. Cathie Nicoll died in 2004, at age ninety-four.

I have met all five. I considered Thompson a mentor and was in a Bible study group with Bentall for several years. The institution with which Nicoll is associated has had a profound effect on my life; that of Hildebrand's has been a significant influence. And I have admired Heppner's musical artistry from afar.

So let's take a look at them one at a time.

Clark Bentall was one of three sons of Charles Bentall, an astute and godly Baptist businessman who built the Bentall construction and development empire in western Canada during the first half of the twentieth century. A cluster of five downtown Vancouver towers immortalizes the Bentall name.

While the business empire has scattered in several non-family directions, the philanthropic interest continues, much of it in or close to Grandview-Calvary Baptist Church in Vancouver's east end, where the three boys learned their spiritual ABCs.

Clark Bentall's Order of Canada officer citation particularly noted that he was a "committed church member" and a redoubtable fundraiser regarded for his advisory role with the Salvation Army's annual campaign.

My recollection was of watching and listening to him in our Bible study group. He asked incisive questions that cut through the spiritual woolliness. He had a keen, natural and basic understanding of Christian ethics. Also, like many successful Christian business people with an engineering background, he was practical. I recall his defence of the sale of the old church of which he was a member, when a new one was built. The building was sold to a branch of Christendom that had a somewhat different theology than that known to Baptists. Some denominational leaders were critical of the deal. "But it was a clean, cash sale," he stated simply.

His defence indicated that the sale, uncomplicated as it was, permitted the church to get on with its ministry, something that it has done both before and since his death. That church is Trinity Baptist, on Vancouver's heavily travelled Granville Street. Its sign, graced with pithy biblical advice that's changed weekly, is read each day by thousands of commuters.

Ben Heppner was a youth pastor in the Christian and Missionary Alliance when he sensed that God wanted him to develop his voice. He is known today as one of the world's great tenors, and his Order of Canada officer citation notes that. It also points out that Heppner does benefit concerts for such organizations as Mennonite Economic Development Associates (MEDA). MEDA is an excellent outlet for Mennonite business people who want to do development projects based on their understanding of the way in which Christian faith and business practices should intersect.

Henry Hildebrand lives in Clearbrook, BC, but the Briercrest Family of Schools, which he founded in the early twentieth century, has shaped the lives of thousands of Canadian young people. His Order of Canada citation simply stressed his role in Christian education. The fact is that Briercrest is just one of the Bible-based colleges that has influenced the west politically, culturally and sociologically in such a way that historians ignore them at their peril.

All Inter-Varsity Christian Fellowship people who work in the organization's Pioneer Camps have summer nicknames. Catherine (Cathie) Nicoll's camp name was "Nicky."

Her citation is more specific than Hildebrand's in implying the relationship of faith to other issues. She is noted for her leadership training work that was seen as helping to develop young people in their appreciation of the environment, music, literature and excellence.

Many IVers recall her as a fine teacher, an excellent

expositor of Scripture who never failed to help her spiritual progeny to see ways to apply the Bible in real life.

Thompson was a man of many parts. In Canada, he was best known as one of the four political leaders who were part of the "house of minorities" of the 1960s. The others were Lester Pearson and John Diefenbaker, who replaced each other as prime minister and opposition leader respectively, and Tommy Douglas.

A former missionary who had helped rebuild Ethiopia's school system after World War II, Thompson became leader of the national Social Credit party. That provided his entrance into federal politics and his opportunity to hold the balance of power in the House of Commons.

An aside with respect to that "house of minorities" was that all four of the leaders were reasonably devout Protestants with a range of evangelical leanings. Thompson and Pearson used to pray together in the latter's office. When Pearson, who won the Nobel peace prize for his diplomatic acumen, needed a troubleshooter in Africa, he sent the former missionary on more than one occasion.

In Thompson's Order of Canada citation, Trinity Western University, World Vision and Samaritan's Purse are mentioned. He played a significant role in all three. In fact, when Franklin Graham, Billy's son, first became involved in Christian Third-World development work, he was firmly advised to take on as a mentor "a fellow up in Canada" who knew the field backward and forward. Graham took that advice, to his continuing benefit.

One other name came to light after I wrote the above, and his story appeared in "doing politics christianly..." #39, written just three days before 9/11. It permitted me not only to write about one more evangelical admitted to the Order of Canada but to explore some of the spiritual and sociological discussions surrounding the ministry in which he is involved.

Questions that Never Occurred to my Grandparents' Doctors

In response to last week's "doing politics christianly..." on past recipients of the Order of Canada, I received a kind note from Brian Stiller, president of Tyndale College and Seminary and former president of the Evangelical Fellowship of Canada. He suggested that I might want to consider his brother, Calvin Stiller, for addition to my list of five Order of Canada members "who have gone before."

Stiller is a London, Ontario immunologist who founded Transplant International. He has been in the forefront of the Organ Donor Card program, which encourages people to sign cards that will permit certain of their organs – heart, kidneys or lungs, for example – to be transplanted in case of unexpected death. It was for his organ donor advocacy that he was honoured with membership in the Order of Canada.

As it happens, he is an evangelical Christian who worships at North Park Community Church, a large and influential congregation with historic Christian Brethren roots, located in suburban London. He quietly admits at times to the belief that his transplant advocacy grows out of his Christian faith and his surgeon's respect for the sanctity of life.

There is, however, a body of opinion within the pro-life movement that is cautionary toward the concept of organ transplants. The point at issue with such people is that a person who has been declared brain dead may not be dead enough, so to speak, to make it ethically acceptable to take his or her organs for transplant.

The philosophical and theological views that drive that particular perspective show in some other ways as well. I will cite and try to synthesize three different outcroppings of those views:

- The linking of contraception and abortion in the debate over how and when anti-abortion legislation should be enacted. *Some pro-life leaders maintain that contraception and abortion are inextricably linked. They suggest that any government elected on a pro-life platform, for example, would be derelict to the cause if it did not include reference to contraception in any anti-abortion legislation it was seeking to enact.*

- The cautionary notes developing in the embryonic stem cell research debate. *The pro-life position, stripped of any caveat, maintains that a government elected on a pro-life platform would be unfaithful to that commitment if it approves of embryonic stem cell use that would save lives. Pro-life adherents reject the validity of the "lesser of two evils" argument — that the life of a dying person is of as much value as the life of an embryo.*

- The maintaining of the idea that dialogue with people who are personally opposed to abortion but ambivalent on the matter of choice represents an unacceptable compromise. *People who maintain this position believe that a government elected on a pro-life platform must enact no compromise legislation, because not to do so would represent an unnecessary capitulation to an anti-life position.*

I hope that I have communicated the above views in a fair and balanced manner. If I have, there seems to be a basis for understanding why Christians engaged in political action get into conflict on these issues.

The fact is that the questions raised here never would have occurred in a thousand years to the doctors who served the grandparents of many of my readers. But today, because of the various facets of the pro-life debate, they become of concern not only to doctors like Calvin Stiller but to leaders of political parties.

Understandably, the concern of the political leaders comes in how to deal with advocacy groups whose objectives include taking hold of a party's apparatus in order to effect the changes they want. One option is to say, "Help me get to be prime minister and I will enact your views into legislation. Period. Full stop." Another is to suggest, "I respect and agree with your viewpoint. Help me to create a situation in which our viewpoint can be debated and can win the respect it deserves. Give me the space I need to work with people who may differ in small or large measure to see if we can find some principled common ground." Yet a third way would be to say, "I don't want to be prime minister if it means subjecting these views to a consensus process. Let's work together to keep this party small and tight, with only one set of views on this issue. We may not have power, but we have the benefit of knowing that we have not altered our views to win a place in a bigger tent."

Chapter Sixteen

One of the Three

Occasionally I refer to the Evangelical Fellowship of Canada as a significant influence on the body politic, from the Christian perspective, along with the Canadian Council of Churches and the Canadian Conference of Catholic Bishops.

This piece, "doing politics christianly..." #48, was filed November 15, 2001, and marked the fifth anniversary of the establishment of the EFC's Centre for Faith and Public Life office in Ottawa.

CHANGING VIEW: KEEPING FOCUS

When the Centre for Faith and Public Life started five years ago, its key people, Bruce Clemenger and Janet Epp Buckingham, had a great view of the Peace Tower and the offices beneath it. Those offices were often the targets of their perceived mandate to be spokespersons for three million Canadians.

In the spring of 2003, Bruce Clemenger was named president of the EFC, succeeding Gary Walsh, who had moved to Seattle to assume the presidency of Interdev. It was a natural move: Interdev is an organization committed to encouraging the development of "ministry partnerships" — the means by which Christian ministries could "do better together what is more difficult to do separately." Walsh had introduced many of Interdev's partnership approaches to the EFC, and they continue to be carried out by Aileen Van Ginkel, the organization's director of ministry empowerment.

Walsh subsequently returned to Toronto to head up Opportunity International Canada, an evangelical agency specializing in micro-enterprise and micro-credit assistance in several less developed countries.

When the good folk across the street built Tower Two of the World Exchange Centre, the view was gone. But that was not why they moved around to the back (south side) of 130 Albert Street. The real reason was that their operation was growing in direct proportion to the increasing influence of the Evangelical Fellowship of Canada as a credible representative of a major sector of Canadian Christianity.

That the EFC has come a long way since its founding in 1964 was evidenced two weeks ago when some 300 religious leaders came, on their own hook, to help celebrate the Centre's fifth anniversary.

As a Christian religious influence on and around the Hill, the EFC is still pretty much a new kid on the block. The Canadian Council of Churches and the Canadian Conference of Catholic Bishops — and their predecessor organizations — had traditionally kept an eye on the place for Canadian Christians from well back into the first half of the twentieth century. However, the EFC became increasingly aware of both its potential collective clout and its distinctiveness from other kinds of Christians. A Hill presence was a natural development.

Clemenger later pleasantly chided me for using the term "clout." The EFC, he suggested, does not like to push its weight around. I assured him I would let my readers know that it was my expression, not his.

The Evangelical Fellowship is an umbrella group for thirty-eight denominations, as well as a few dozen "parachurch" organizations and several hundred mainline Protestant congregations. Among the member denominations are various kinds of Baptist, Mennonite, Pentecostal, Reformed and Holiness groups. In addition, Presbyterians and Anglicans have observer status at EFC deliberations.

The EFC estimates a constituency of some three million. Its leaders suggest that these are the Protestants who answer the pollsters "evangelically." They affirm such core beliefs as the deity of Jesus, the authority of the Bible and the validity of being "born again." About two million Catholics would answer almost the same way.

The EFC provides the kind of leadership one expects of a multi-church organization as it grows to maturity. It has developed a cluster of directors that includes the aforementioned Clemenger and Epp Buckingham.

Brian Stiller, who preceded Gary Walsh as EFC president, had both the temperament and appetite to take the EFC from twenty years as a mainly voluntary organization to a professional unit with many of the characteristics of an advocacy or quasi-legislative group.

A Pentecostal minister who ran Youth for Christ for several years, Stiller always had a fair understanding of political influence and the potential for religious faith to shape it. When the head job at the EFC came open in the early eighties, he jumped at it, knowing he would be taking the then insular fellowship into new areas of political activism.

He did a couple of things to trigger the changes. He criss-crossed Canada with a workshop he designed called Understanding our Times. *In his sessions he talked about how evangelical churches had previously concentrated on evangelism and left the political and social action to the mainstream Protestants and Catholics.*

Stiller explored the roles of the second prime minister, devout Baptist Alexander Mackenzie, and evangelical mayors who gave the village by the lake the title of "Toronto the Good." He spoke of the evangelical influences in the temperance movement and the abolition of slavery. He also developed a lively leadership magazine called Faith Today, *which is still affectionately dubbed "the evangelical* Maclean's.*"*

The capping of his work was the establishing of the Centre for Faith and Public Affairs, giving the evangelical movement an Ottawa presence that had been, at best, elusive from the EFC's headquarters in downtown Markham.

As the new EFC president, Clemenger is, for now at least, keeping his office in Ottawa, rather than moving to the Markham office.

Clemenger and Epp Buckingham, the EFC's legal counsel, keep a running stream of briefs to cabinet ministers and commons committees. Their latest was to the justice and human rights committee, with comment on the proposed Bill C-36, Justice Minister Anne McLellan's anti-terrorism legislation. A major point of the brief: make the legislation clear that providing humanitarian assistance or engaging in other charitable purposes is not criminalized.

Epp Buckingham and Clemenger maintain that the difficulty for evangelical organizations engaged in relief and development work in hot spots is that they have to do their work in settings where terrorism may be the order of the day. They may even give medical aid to terrorists who are living in neighbourhoods where the agencies are working. Where does Christian social action stop and the abetting of terrorism start? And what does that mean for those parts of Bill C-36 that attempt to deal with money laundering and the control of charities that really are fronts for terrorist activities?

Leading and speaking for evangelicals can be a bit like herding cats. Aileen van Ginkel, director of EFC's "ministry empowerment" department, brings together groups of EFC members into consultations and round tables to find ways of working in what is called "ministry partnerships" in such areas as political action, media and higher education.

During one recent consultation involving Christian radio, television and newspaper types, much of the animated and, at times, somewhat combative hallway discussion concerned the relative religious merits of Stockwell Day and the Democratic Representatives.

EFC member denominations run the gamut in matters such as female ordination, where to draw the line on gay rights, right/left politics and economics, social justice, pluralism and the estimated timing of the second coming of Christ. Their emphasis on personal responsibility before God skews them right on many social and economic issues, however.

Depending on how widely the net is drawn, Clemenger and Epp Buckingham estimate fifty to seventy-five people in the House of Commons are evangelicals and fellow travellers. Among the Liberals, John Manley, David Kilgour, John McKay and Paul Steckle are the most likely to turn up at evangelically-spawned networking opportunities. Elsie Wayne is the lone Tory in the camp, although the new

PC-DR caucus has the benefit of four DRs who are known evangelicals: Chuck Strahl, Val Merideth, Deb Grey and Grant McNally. There are about twenty-five evangelicals in the main Alliance caucus.

Almost all the DRs, including the four aforementioned evangelicals, returned to the Alliance caucus when Stephen Harper became the leader. It can be safely noted that much of the subsequent healing of the party division came through the practice of a fair amount of Christian-style reconciliation concepts. Chuck Strahl, particularly, who was deputy leader of the PC-DR caucus, was utilized as a point person by Harper to liaison with Peter MacKay in the lead up to the merger of the two parties.

Slightly Baptist Alexa McDonough and United Church minister Bill Blaikie are the most likely among the NDP to keep in touch with at least the left wing of evangelicalism. Daniel Turp, a former Bloc MP defeated in the last election, is a serious Presbyterian who liked to joke that his Scots brothers and sisters in the faith argue eloquently for the separation of Scotland from England.

So the cat herding continues, and the EFC sees no end of work in interpreting the good news to the felines on the Hill.

Chapter Seventeen

To Speak or Not to Speak: What Was the Question?

What can a Christian say or do or not say or do in the public square? At times, that battle has raged around the Hill. Some of the combatants have been participants in what have been termed the "culture wars."

The primary premise of "culture war" theory is that we are on a slippery slope headed for the day when one might expect to be thrown in jail for speaking explicitly about his or her Christian faith. I would not want to kick that theory in the teeth, but I tend generally to be more optimistic.

I believe a certain spin was put on the military chaplaincy controversy that erupted in 2002. It was instigated by people who wanted us to know that a muzzle had been placed on the chaplains by bureaucrats whose influences extended into the prime minister's office.

Again, I do not want to deny that there were anti-Christian people in the structures who wanted to shut out Christians. But that was not the whole story. In November 2001, "doing politics christianly..." #50 and #51 provided a different, and more optimistic, slant on the issue.

Lloyd Mackey

SAINTS IN CAESAR'S HOUSEHOLD

When the news stories about Christianity being forbidden in military religious services began popping up last week, it was a bit mystifying, especially since I had been taking note of Commodore Timothy Maindonald's efforts to recognize evangelical Christianity as an increasingly significant part of the religious life of the Canadian Forces.

Maindonald is an Anglican minister and military chaplain who has recently assumed the CF's chaplain-general role. Rick Hiebert, editor of the Pentecostal Testimony, *wrote a story about the commodore's particular gesture toward evangelicalism.*

When Maindonald became chaplain-general last August, he made the point that he wished to be installed in an evangelical church rather than, as had usually been the case, in a Catholic or Anglican cathedral. In fact, he approached Pentecostal minister Stewart Hunter, a member of the interfaith committee on Canadian Military Chaplaincy, to help him find a venue for the installation service.

The place chosen was 1,200-seat Bethel Pentecostal Church in Nepean, an Ottawa suburb.

Captain Pierre Bergeron told Hiebert that such a thing would have been unthinkable ten years ago. Himself a Pentecostal cleric, Bergeron noted that Christian chaplaincy slots, formerly filled by Catholics and mainline Protestants, now draw ministers from such groups as Free Methodist and Associated Gospel denominations.

In light of such a nod toward churches that believe in unabashedly sharing and spreading the Good News, how could the new chaplain-general be accused of shutting out their ability to communicate their distinctives – such as the divinity of Jesus, the authority of Scripture and the validity of the new birth?

Such was not quite the case, however.

The confusion began when Colonel Ron Bourque, top Catholic CF chaplain, allegedly told a Kingston Whig-Standard *reporter that chaplains were forbidden from using such phrases as "Father, Son and Holy Spirit" in prayers offered at military services.*

After the story "got legs" and it became a point of contention on the floor of the House of Commons, Colonel Bourque sent word to Leon Benoit, the official opposition defence critic, that he had been misquoted.

My guess would be that he was probably not directly misquoted but his words may have been taken out of context in a reporter's attempt to make the issue simple enough to get the attention of readers. That, indeed, is one of the occupational hazards in both journalism and advocacy work.

These are the facts, as indicated in the directive in question from the CF's chaplaincy branch:

- *In voluntary worship, as well as in ecumenical or interfaith worship where a number of religious leaders are participating, chaplains may conduct themselves in accordance with their own denominational traditions.*
- *In a public ceremony involving various faith groups where the chaplain is the sole representative of all faith groups, prayers normally should be "inclusive" and celebrants are encouraged to be "sensitive in the use of specific sacred faith formulas."*

There was nothing in the Whig-Standard *that actually contradicted the directive. But nothing, either, that places Christianity under attack.*

However, Captain Swavek Gorniak, a Catholic chaplain at Kingston's Royal Military College, acknowledges that "it is difficult to make changes because if you don't say what people…are used to hearing, they will say that you are not orthodox enough, that you are not Christian enough.

"We are going into uncharted territory here."

A look at the mirror image of this situation takes us to a piece appearing in Saturday's National Post *(November 24, 2001), entitled "When does foreign aid work become evangelism?"*

Writer Marina Jimenez talks about Heather Mercer and Dayna Curry, the two Texans who were among the eight Christian relief and development workers jailed by the Taliban in Afghanistan for spreading Christianity.

Jimenez provides the Texans' take on their experience and quotes, as well, from World Vision Canada's president, David Toycen, about what aid workers in alien cultures need to keep in mind about sharing their faith. Curry allowed that they were "partly guilty" of the "crimes" they were accused of committing.

"I did make a copy of a book with stories about Jesus in English and Farsi and gave it to a friend who had asked for it. We also showed a film about Jesus to some people. In Islamic countries, the issue of faith is a top priority. They shared their religious beliefs with us and also asked us about our own religion. That was our defense."

Sounds just fine, at least in the context of North American pluralism.

Toycen notes, however, that in working in Afghanistan, "Those of us from a faith-based perspective must be sensitive not to use foreign aid as a manipulation to enforce hungry people to embrace our view of life or profession of faith."

Jimenez offers the observation that "the road from [Texas] to Kabul is not as long nor as complicated as it may seem. The Taliban's belief that God's word is above man's law, that it is noble to die for your religion, is close to the evangelical Christian belief that the law of Christ is the ultimate word and that Christians are compelled to bear witness to their faith, even in hostile environments."

I think Jimenez oversimplifies. While most evangelical aid workers would agree with her last statement, only a small subset would press the point to martyrdom or the persecution of non-Christians. Most would likely take Toycen's part, especially if they believe that they are in it for the long haul.

There was some feedback from "doing politics christianly…" #50 that resulted in the following week's piece, which introduced the additional element of a response to a column written in the *Calgary Sun* by its editor, Licia Corbella, a very effective and discerning journalist who happens to be a serious Christian.

WHICH ONE IS TELLING THE TRUTH?

I had an interesting call from Alberta last week in response to "doing politics christianly…" #50, entitled "Saints in Caesar's Household," which explored the current directives for Canadian Forces chaplains.

The caller told me someone had forwarded to her my piece along with a press release from an advocacy group commenting on the same issue. The covering note rhetorically asked which one was telling the truth, and that was the question the caller was posing to me.

You may recall that the furor over the alleged attempts to get chaplains to delete Jesus had mystified me, because the new chaplain-general had especially extended himself to Pentecostals and other evangelicals in arranging for his installation to take place in a Pentecostal church. And I don't know of any group of people less likely to want to leave Jesus out of a prayer.

Perhaps my answer to the caller will indicate my inclination to draw a line between advocacy and analysis. Advocacy involves groups that raise issues on which political leaders can take stands. Analysis hopefully explores various sides of an issue, even those facets that might weaken one side or another of the advocates' arguments.

The particular advocate's press release, to which the caller drew my attention, pointed to the "delete Jesus contention," the prayerless September 11 memorial on Parliament Hill and the order to leave Jesus out of the prayers at Peggy's Cove three years ago, after Swissair Flight 111 went down. It cited these three incidents as examples of a government-directed drift toward "politically correct" secular domination in Canadian society.

Was it true?

I was not going to argue with the caller. Instead, I put forward a couple of additional facts that could be taken into account in arriving at an opinion.

With respect to the Swissair issue, I suggested that, if the chaplain-general's directive had been used at the time, the issue would not have been raised, because there were clergy at Peggy's Cove from several different faiths. Thus, each minister could act freely within his or her own denominational tradition, and none could be fairly criticized for using the name of Jesus.

With regard to the Parliament Hill memorial, one little-known fact is that Prime Minister Chrétien was invited to a memorial mass immediately following the event. Indeed, invited is probably a weak word. Art Babych, at the time Canadian Catholic News Parliament Hill reporter, told me that Ottawa Catholic Archbishop Marcel Gervais told Chrétien, in effect, to "be there!" at Notre Dame Cathedral, a three-minute limo ride from the Hill.

More to the point, perhaps, the September 11 tragedy spawned dozens of interdenominational and interfaith services across Canada. The church where we were members for about fifteen years, First Baptist in Vancouver, was publicized nationwide for opening its doors to hundreds of people who needed spiritual leadership during that time.

In response to a note from another journalist, I suggested that a certain amount of common sense must come into these matters. If, for example, a Catholic chaplain should invoke Mary at an interdenominational service, or a Pentecostal cleric try to get the gathered group to speak in tongues, their superiors might raise a few eyebrows. In a military regimen, the leaders are cautious about surprises, and that should not be considered unreasonable.

Which brings up Licia Corbella's otherwise excellent column in the December 2 issue of the Calgary Sun. Parenthetically, I commend her writing. She is a warm Christian who shares her faith most competently and, at times, movingly, in a secular context. To read her, and Sun Media's many other columnists, go to the Canoe.com site, click on "newspapers" then "columnists."

I pause here to comment on how Licia Corbella became a Christian and the very indirect but personally satisfying role that involved yours truly. Licia and her then husband-to-be came to faith in 1984, at the Billy Graham mission in Vancouver. She has written from time to time about how that commitment changed her life. Her writing demonstrates the ability to bring faith to the public square with integrity while continuing to be true to her work as the editor of a major Canadian daily.

My side of the story is that I was the secretary of the executive committee of the Vancouver Billy Graham mission. The story behind that story was that a group of Vancouver Christians had begun to explore the possibility of having the evangelist there a few years before and ended up with the fulfilling task of testing the waters among Christian leaders and putting together the invitation. Sometimes one wonders if the time spent on a particular project—in this case, the Billy Graham mission—is worthwhile. Much of my journalism career has been spent attempting to develop younger Christian journalists. So it is fulfilling now to know that one of the best was not developed through my work but came to faith because a group of us were able to help pull together a significant evangelism project.

A story came to Corbella's attention about a chaplain who prayed "in the strong name of Jesus" for a cadet who came to him complaining of an evil spirit visiting him at night as he slept. The prayer worked so well the cadet's platoon commander commended the chaplain, but his own superior officer chastised him.

My gentle suggestion is that the chastisement was not specifically for the use of the strong name of Jesus but, more likely, for practising exorcism.

Now exorcism is an honoured, if somewhat controversial, practice in many Catholic and Pentecostal circles, and its practitioners maintain that invoking Jesus' name is essential to the process.

Undoubtedly, some military chaplains feel the need to know what kinds of prayer therapy are going on under their commands. After all, there are both psychological and spiritual issues involved in some of those situations.

My sense is that faith is alive and well in many parts of the land where we might have thought it had died and gone to heaven. That does not detract from the need for advocacy groups to raise issues surrounding the place of faith in public life. Some will do so to advance the cause for the Christianizing of society's major institutions. Some encourage individuals and groups to let their faith permeate the way they live so others will want the Jesus they have. The difference between the two approaches shows up in the way groups build and present their cases.

Listen carefully and check out the contexts when you read of or hear an advocacy group at work. That care will pay off when you come to shaping your own faith for usefulness in the political sphere.

Chapter Eighteen

Andy Savoy Puts His Ear to the Ground

The Parliamentary Library publishes a collection of news clippings several times a week for the use of members of the press gallery. Most often the clippings are drawn from the major national and large city dailies; occasionally they come from some of the smaller regional newspapers.

One morning, there was a short story from the *New Brunswick Telegraph-Journal*, the province's leading regional paper. It talked about Andy Savoy, a rookie Liberal MP in Tobique-Mactaquac, a rural riding north of Fredericton. The story told that he was pulling together a group of ministers and other religious leaders to advise him on issues where faith might have some input.

This excerpt from "doing politics christianly..." #54, written just before Christmas 2001, talks about Andy Savoy's "spiritual committee."

A "Spiritual Committee" in New Brunswick's "Bible Belt"

The December 19 New Brunswick Telegraph Journal *included an item headlined "Rookie MP establishes 'spiritual committee.'" The member in question is Andy Savoy, Liberal MP for Tobique-Mactaquac, described by the* Telegraph Journal *as the province's "Bible belt."*

Savoy is not sure that the term is quite accurate. Yet he notes: "A lot of politicians don't like to mix politics and religion, but the religious community is such a strong part of my riding that I feel it should have a voice."

As a journalist who practised most of his craft in BC's Fraser Valley until moving to Ottawa, I was curious to find out exactly what an east coast Bible belt was like.

In the Fraser Valley, the dominant churches are Mennonite, Alliance, Christian Reformed and Pentecostal. Some of those churches attract congregations of 2,000 or more. The valley is also headquarters to Trinity Western University, Campus Crusade and Focus on the Family, as well as BC Christian News.

Fortunately, Edna and I were able to take our first trip to Atlantic Canada last summer and travelled right through Savoy's riding, staying in Woodstock, its largest city. So I was able to envisage the physical surroundings: small cities in a picturesque river valley, lots of food processing plants, sawmills and pulp mills.

And lots of well-kept churches, mostly of the Protestant variety, except in French-speaking towns, where the Catholic spires lift high.

Savoy is establishing a "spiritual advisory committee" as one of several intended to give him input on issues of major import to the riding. The others are agriculture, forestry, transportation, social/family and recreation/tourism. He allows that the people advising him on the social/family committee may bring some faith perspectives to bear, as well.

In most of the English-speaking portions of the riding,

the main churches are Baptist, Wesleyan, Pentecostal and Presbyterian, with Anglican, Lutheran, United and Catholic close behind. In some towns, the Seventh Day Adventists and Mormons are present in substantial numbers as well.

In Hartland, site of the world's longest covered bridge, New Brunswick Bible Institute is a social influence with which to be reckoned. In Florence, the main thing is the big McCain's food processing plant. The McCain family has been long noted for its Presbyterian leanings.

Savoy, for his part, is a United Church person married to a Catholic. He and his wife are raising their two children, aged two and seven months, as Catholics. He describes himself as a "practising Christian" who has a high regard for Preston Manning and the way he has related faith and politics. At thirty-eight, he is an engineer by profession and developed his taste for politics as a town councillor in Perth-Andover, where he lives, in the south end of the riding.

Savoy would not be in the House of Commons if it were not for the Tory–Alliance vote-splitting in the last election. He beat the Tory incumbent by about 150 votes. The Alliance candidate was only another 100 or so behind, on a vote total of around 40,000.

Savoy recognizes that there are probably more serious Christians in the riding who voted for his two main opponents in last year's election than voted for him. With respect to his spiritual advisory committee, his strategy is to throw wide the invitational net to ministers and other key religious leaders throughout the riding. He plans a forum in mid-January [2002] and promises to report back to me on how it worked out when he returns to Ottawa late that month.

Savoy intends to facilitate the forum himself and to "ask lots of questions and take lots of notes." He is well aware that the spiritual advice he gets from some people attending the forum will be different from what he will get from others. But he believes, as well, that there will be common threads and complementary positions stated. He also knows that his riding has very few people who belong to religions other than some form of Christianity. The advice he gets is not binding, but he recognizes that he ignores it at his political peril.

Andy Savoy may be one of the few MPs who actually formalizes his arrangements with a multi-denominational committee. But most who have any Christian background at all know that part of keeping in touch with constituents has to involve listening to those who give religious leadership in their communities.

I reported earlier on the Pastors' Council, the group of megachurch pastors who periodically visit Ottawa to meet with cabinet ministers, other MPs and senators — on request.

The Andy Savoy story runs in the opposite direction. It involves a proactive MP networking with the Christian leaders in his riding. The sociology is different from that involving the megachurch ministers. There are few, if any, megachurches in most of the New Brunswick "Bible belt" ridings. Most of the churches are small-town congregations with perhaps 100 to 500 people each. The Catholic parishes may be larger, but multiple staffing and thousands of people converging on a weekend at one church building is not part of the picture.

Nevertheless, many of the churches are virile and influential in their communities. That is why it is important for MPs like Andy Savoy to listen to their "spiritual committees."

Chapter Nineteen

The Cabinet Minister, the Creator and the Mormons

In this chapter, I want to introduce three Christian-based spiritual elements around the Hill with which few evangelicals Christians would be acquainted.

This situation has little to do with direct theological conflict, although some evangelicals of a more fundamentalist leaning might accuse me of syncretism in even introducing either or all of the elements.

The first piece, "doing politics christianly..." #52, was written December 12, 2001.

THE ENCASEMENT OF THE CREATOR

The Honourable Ethel Blondin-Andrew is the secretary of state for children and youth, in Jean Chrétien's cabinet. The Liberal member for the Western Arctic, she comes from the aboriginal Dene nation and, according to a recent interviewer, is a "very strong Christian."

Insofar as this piece is concerned, the story actually begins with John McKay. He is, among other things, Liberal member for Scarborough East, co-founder of the Canadian Christian Legal Fellowship, current chair of the National

Prayer Breakfast and an active "servant leader" at Spring Garden Baptist Church, an influential evangelical congregation in mid-town Toronto.

McKay's wife's name is Carolyn Dartnell. She is a producer-interviewer for "Insight," a well-done faith-based magazine show running on VISION-TV.

Telling me about the interview she conducted with Blondin-Andrew, Dartnell made the point that her subject is a "very strong Christian." Having now been able to preview the clip, I concur, but not for the usual orthodox reasons.

Blondin-Andrew has drawn strength from the Catholicism she grew up with and lives and breathes within the tenets of that faith. She is also careful not to reject every aspect of what, in the Caucasian world, is often called "native spirituality."

"The Creator is the Creator. It does not matter how the Creator is encased. Nothing changes who and what the Creator is." That is a quick paraphrase of what Blondin-Andrew has to say about the raw material of her God stance.

She has good and not so good things to say about residential schools. She speaks disarmingly, and seemingly without regret, of the fact that, as a young woman, she had three children while she was yet unmarried. They are all in their twenties and thirties, and she is very proud of them.

In aboriginal tradition, she has gone hunting with her husband. And, in the interview, she successfully contrasts the Dene lifestyle with the sophistication of large city life in Canada.

Blondin-Andrew speaks of the love and healing that took place in her marriage of ten years, in part because she had her husband charged with assault in their early time together.

He actually served time for that offence. Now, however, she affirms that he has become the man he was meant to be.

Before I ended that particular piece, I added some comments about the Canadian Alliance leadership race that ended in Stephen Harper's becoming the party's leader. All four contenders for the leadership were evangelical Christians except one, Grant Hill, an Alberta physician, father of seven, antique car aficionado—and Mormon.

The possibility of Grant Hill's run is intriguing. He is not an evangelical but a Mormon. Party insiders interested in encouraging him to run have been curious to know how that would impact on his ability to get along with evangelicals. From this perch, the analysis is that in Alliance, Reform and Social Credit politics, both in Alberta and nationally, Mormons and evangelicals have gotten along well because, although they differ sharply on theology, they have very similar cultural and lifestyle values.

In more recent times, Stephen Covey, father of the "principle-centred leadership" concept, and Christianity Today magazine have played a role in building those relationships.

Hill did not win, but he remains well-respected in the upper echelons of the CA. However, his presence in the race revealed a long-standing "Alberta reality" in both provincial and federal politics.

Because of the "oil patch," Alberta is likely the most American of all Canadian provinces. Many Americans move to Alberta to work in the patch and to engage in ranching and other similar "Western" proclivities.

Many of those Americans are evangelicals. A fair

number of Mormons as well came to their particular faith through the conversion efforts that were part of the Latter Day Saints' contribution to the building of the American West. The Mormon influence has always represented a strong and respected minority influence in Alberta politics, in the Social Credit, Conservative, Reform and Canadian Alliance parties. More than evangelicals, even, they are seen as clean-living, morally upright, God-fearing, pro-life, family values people.

At the same time, the evangelical Bible colleges on the prairies have usually included courses on the Mormons, Jehovah's Witnesses, Christian Scientists and, in the past, Seventh Day Adventists. Those courses have generally categorized such groups as "cults" and practitioners of deviant theology — no matter their fine attributes.

In due course, the SDAs were usually dropped from the cult list because reforms within their own group brought them closer into line with traditional evangelical theology, and they had a thing or two to teach evangelicals, as well, about health and Third-World development.

The JWs and Christian Scientists were fewer in number and did not really show up on the evangelical radar. However, especially in southern Alberta where a major Mormon Temple is located near Lethbridge, in Cardston, the Mormons were numerous enough to make a difference in elections. Their prowess meant that they had energy to spare in their commitment to community and political service.

Fast forward to today, and we see Grant Hill and Stephen Covey as interesting examples of the way in which Mormons and evangelicals in both Canada and the United States see themselves as competitors, rather than enemies. In those relationships, they eye each other with care, maintain their distinctive doctrines in their respective churches and co-operate in community and political work where it can be done without rancour.

The reference in the preceding "doing politics christianly..." to Stephen Covey and *Christianity Today* magazine provides a contemporary context for the scenario of the Canadian political Mormons in the CA. In February 2000, *CT* ran a major feature about the reconciliation project run by a Pentecostal church in Provo, Utah, a small city in the Mormon heartland near Salt Lake City. In brief, the project was to build relationships between Pentecostals and Mormons, the latter of which represented ninety percent of the community's population. A key figure on the Mormon side of the project was Stephen Covey, whose books and seminars on "principle-centred" leadership and lifestyle have been widely accepted by religious people across the spectrum, including evangelicals.

In that setting, the *CT* report on the project communicated the message that evangelicals and Mormons could live and let live together in such a community. In effect, the reconciliation involved not only improving relations between leaders and people in the two groups but reconciling the reality that there would always be these competing entities.

In the Alberta/Canada/CA context, Grant Hill is the resident Mormon. He won his crack at the permanent leadership of the CA because, as interim leader after Stockwell Day resigned, he held the parliamentary caucus together and kept relations with the dissidents from deteriorating into cold-blooded political genocide.

He was trusted because he understood both the political and religious culture of what was going on in the party, but he was not an "insider." Mormons know better than to become insiders. A close study of James Dobson's Focus on the Family organization will show that Mormons are strong supporters of FOTF, but they do not try to take over and capture its culture for themselves.

The names of many influential Alberta-based Mormon political figures could be noted, but I will mention just one more, Solon Low, who led the national Social Credit party in the House of Commons in the early 1950s, before evangelical Robert Thompson took over.

We will move now to a consideration of a group whose office has been about 500 feet from mine, near Parliament Hill, but about which I knew little until the day described below in a "Capital Views" column that appeared in the December 2002 issue of *ChristianCurrent*.

THE STILL SMALL VOICE OF ARCHIE MACKENZIE

It was the anniversary date of the founding of the United Nations. An energetic retired dentist rapidly approaching his ninetieth birthday was briskly walking me across town to listen to a luncheon speech by another man, who was to turn eighty-seven that week.

The second man was Archie Mackenzie. As I listened to him, something clicked in my mind. I knew I had met him once before.

Ever since he retired from the British diplomatic service, Mackenzie has roamed the world, encouraging diplomats and politicians to build their professional and personal lives on the standards of honesty, purity, unselfishness and love. In addition, for practical purposes, he urged them to try to seek God's will each morning through the vehicle of a "quiet time."

Occasionally, he would stop by in Victoria to see the now-late Mel Smith, a lawyer and a staunch Plymouth Brethren-reared Christian who for thirty years guided BC politicians in the shaping and arguing of constitutional issues.

For his part, Mel would get a few of his Christian friends together to meet Archie (he doesn't mind the informality of such address). They would grill him on his theological views and try to figure out if he was a real Christian. I was privileged to sit in on one of those meetings.

Mel's friends were curious because the cut of Archie's biblical cloth was a bit different. He tended to dwell more on ethical and moral values and a bit less on the theological niceties inbred into the Brethren-Baptist continuum that was Mel's lifelong avocation.

Now, Scots-bred Presbyterian Archie was in Ottawa. He had just written a book called Faith in Diplomacy: a Memoir. *In it, he pretty much lays out his diplomatic adventures and his commitment to those spiritual values he picked up so many years ago at Oxford.*

I have entitled this piece "The Still Small Voice of Archie Mackenzie" because his influence – and that of the movement of which he is a part – is such a contrast to the day-to-day noise that is a part of the, albeit necessary, political advocacy and activism in and around Parliament Hill. The movement was known as Moral Re-Armament or MRA for short.

Recall the biblical story of the prophet Elijah in 1 Kings 19 as he awaits the direction of God in the face of a recalcitrant people. The windstorm came, then the earthquake and the fire. But God was not there, in any of those wonders; he was present in a still, small voice.

Reading Faith in Diplomacy *is like sensing that voice. Indeed, one of the things I learned early in its pages was that*

MRA coined the phrase "quiet time" to refer to that point at the beginning of the day when the Christian quietly tries to find God's direction for the day. That direction is sought through the habitual orderly and logical contemplation of Scripture and quiet prayer in the light of what is happening in the world.

I learned of the practice through Inter-School Christian Fellowship, little knowing that MRA had grandfathered it. The quiet time is still a part of my life – with some high-tech modifications. Edna and I read a portion of Scripture in print form most mornings, but my survey of the major news of the day is on-line.

Today, MRA is known as Initiatives of Change. It continues to do a quiet work in spiritual support for diplomatic initiative at the highest levels.

When Archie Mackenzie and his spiritual kin are at work, key people in the diplomatic and foreign affairs communities, Christian or otherwise, listen with care.

One thing I noticed about the luncheon I attended with my near-nonagenarian friend was that many of its participants were what we younger folk call "a bit long in the tooth." Two active IOC members were retired journalists I knew and respected. But I had no idea this group was part of their spiritual support system.

One senior parliamentarian who is known for his outspoken Christian stance, David Kilgour, takes a keen interest in the activities of IOC. He is also prepared to admit that it helps open doors of understanding in various countries that were in his bailiwick when he was secretary of state for Asia and the Pacific. Kilgour is in his fifties, thus of a generation that has been handed the IOC legacy, and will undoubtedly keep it in focus.

Richard Weeks, the man who runs IOC's Ottawa office, is in his fifties, but those who carry on are hoping, just a little, that they will be able to attract younger people to the movement. So, it was salutary to see three students from the Laurentian Leadership Centre—the Trinity Western University Ottawa presence—at the luncheon and to learn that Mackenzie spent several hours with two dozen LLC students later in the week.

I asked Don Page, the founding director of the LLC who, in an earlier "incarnation," had been a senior policy advisor to several foreign affairs ministers, what MRA/IOC meant to him. He responded that it was, indeed, a quiet but very significant spiritual influence on the Hill and in many capitals throughout the world.

Weeks made the point that, although it was taking on more of a multi-faith hue given the range of religions represented in the leadership particularly of developing nations, it would always draw its ethical and moral basis from the teachings of the Bible.

Chapter Twenty

Responding to the Left and the Right

This next piece was written on New Year's Day 2002. It reflected some thoughts that came out of critiques of previous pieces.

ENTERING A NEW YEAR; LEARNING FROM THE OLD

I heard from two former colleagues during the past couple of weeks. The first I would describe as being a little more liberal, theologically and politically, than I am. The other is somewhat more conservative.

The first-mentioned agreed basically with the thesis of "doing politics christianly..." #55, in which I talked about the spiritual committee New Brunswick Liberal MP Andy Savoy had set up to provide faith-based perspectives from his "Bible belt" riding. My friend wondered, however, why I had suggested that faith perspectives might show themselves in one of several other committees Savoy had set up — that dealing with family and social issues. Why, he asked, had I not thought to mention that faith might be a factor in the deliberations of the forestry, environment and economic committees?

Good question. He is right. The fact is, though, that in recent years, because of the influence of faith-based social conservatism, Christians do not always make the connection between the gospel and economic issues.

Theologically-liberal Christians do keep the issue alive, often to the yawns of their more conservative brothers and sisters. They do so with some success, as the Ecumenical Jubilee Initiative campaign of a couple of years ago has demonstrated. Christian action of the more liberal variety definitely moved former Finance Minister Paul Martin to cancel a lot more of the impoverished nations' debts to Canada than might have happened if it had not been brought to his attention. The same thing happened throughout the other G-8 nations through coordinated ecumenical action.

I should note, too, that theological liberals are not alone in raising awareness regarding a Christian approach to economics, poverty, Third-World development and related issues. Earlier in the year I covered the Hill Lecture by Marvin Olasky, the "compassionate conservative" advisor to President Bush, sponsored by the socially-conservative think-tank, the Centre for Cultural Renewal.

It is entirely likely the influence of such people as Olasky has meant that the whole Afghanistan war was fought much differently than it would have been. That is because the American president included among his advisors people who insisted that the treatment of the Afghan people after the war and the redevelopment of their nation were critical. Compassionate conservatism – or whatever you want to call it – has a contribution to make in giving lie to the insistence of bin Laden and the Taliban that the "infidels" needed destroying.

The other former, and more conservative, colleague asked to be removed from the "doing politics christianly…"

list. He said that as long as I was promoting liberal Protestantism as real Christianity, he could no longer have fellowship with me in the gospel. In effect, he said that when one has to choose between the plain teaching of Scripture and human thinking, the human approach is always wrong.

From this perch, things are not that simple, and I told him so. Here is what I said:

1. Matthew 12:30 says, "He who is not with me is against me." Luke 9:49,50 says, "for whoever is not against you is for you." Both passages have contexts that assist the reader to make decisions as to when to apply one or the other. Application is essential to the process of accepting that Scripture is God-breathed, even when there are seemingly contradictory "plain teachings."

2. You will recall the commendation George Bush received for quoting the Romans passage that says "nothing shall separate us from the love of God." I mentioned at one point about the "Jesus understood" syndrome — Bush left it understood that the rest of the passage said, "which is in Christ Jesus our Lord." Guess which liberal Protestant magazine got the whole thing right — on the front cover of its November 2001 issue. It was the United Church Observer.

A bit of year-end reading brought forward an interesting nugget. Frank Bucholtz is editor of the Langley Times, a three-times-a-week, 40,000 circulation newspaper. LT serves a community with many churches (some among the largest in Canada), Trinity Western University and the Canadian headquarters for both Campus Crusade for Christ and Focus on the Family.

Bucholtz happens to be a serious Christian who has practised his craft in a secular setting for over twenty years. His wife, Bonnie, is also a discerning and capable journalist.

So it was interesting to see his December 28 LT column. He had a disclaimer: his predictions were "more for the sake of going out on a limb than anything else."

He suggested that "Stockwell Day will not be re-elected leader of the Canadian Alliance, despite his best efforts. Instead, the party will be led by a woman, Diane Ablonczy — and she will have the best chance to become Canada's first elected female prime minister."

Now, that is not what I am hearing in Ottawa. Ablonczy, MP for Calgary Nose Hill, is hardly on the leadership radar screen, despite having a sterling debating record in the House of Commons. Some of the central Canada pundits are trying to compare her to Kim Campbell, even suggesting that her leadership and organizational skills are less developed than were those of the short-lived Tory prime minister of 1993. Some of punditry has been, in my view, quite obviously sexist — or at least politically incorrect gender-insensitive, to coin a phrase.

What does Bucholtz know that we don't? I intend to ask him later in the week. Meanwhile, I would suggest that if his prediction is to come true, Ablonczy will require an organization that can match Day's in attracting serious Christian people who want to become involved in politics. Her niche is the part of the evangelical Christian community that never committed to Day but is prepared to park their Tory or Liberal support if someone other than himself shows up as a credible CA leadership candidate.

As it turned out, of course, my hunch was more correct than Bucholtz's. He was right that the winner was not Day, but it was Stephen Harper who took him out, not

Ablonczy. It was Harper's ability to pick up memberships from that very large part of the evangelical CA support base that was not in the Day corner that brought him the margin he needed to win.

I expect that one reason he could pick up that support was that he was not a female. Not that evangelicals are anti-female; they are simply not ready for female leadership—and neither are people of other religions and in other parties. In most cases, the exception proves the rule.

When some interesting journalism on the part of both *ChristianWeek* and *Report* newsmagazine revealed that Harper and Ablonczy were both evangelicals, the tide began to turn. There were some clear indications, indeed, that many supporters signed up by Day recruiters switched to Harper on receipt of the new information about his faith. (Harper receives his pastoral care in Christian and Missionary Alliance Churches in both Calgary and Ottawa, and Ablonczy and her husband are members of the 5,000-strong Centre Street Church in Calgary. Both make their evangelical Christian stance a matter of public record, albeit quietly.)

Ablonczy did commit one deft act before announcing her run for the CA leadership. She visited Joe Clark, told him what she wanted to say and asked for his feedback. He gave it and in the process seemed genuinely appreciative of her gesture. He gave her no endorsement. Indeed, he is not in a position to do so. She made no promises to him; neither should she have.

However, in communicating with the Tory leader, she tacitly acknowledged that, like it or not, Clark is still a player in the centre-right political game. Conciliatory politics requires that kind of avowal. It may be that Bucholtz — unwittingly or otherwise — has figured something out.

The Tories got a new leader to succeed Joe Clark. Peter MacKay was variously tagged as being interested in working with Stephen Harper and as trying to keep away from him. The fact is that there were enormous tensions within the Conservative party between some of the younger crowd who want to work out a coalition with the Alliance and those in the older sector who want to bring CA supporters into the grand old party of Sir John A.

MacKay dealt with those tensions as best he could. And, in due course, with the help of senior "emissaries" from both parties—at least three of them seriously Christian—Harper and MacKay were able to bring the Alliance and Conservative parties together.

We will talk about Joe Clark and Preston Manning in the next chapter, now that they are both senior statespersons in their respective parts of the political spectrum.

Chapter Twenty-One

Resurrecting an Old Blueprint

One of the small untold stories about Joe Clark's long-time friendship with Preston Manning was about the very gracious speech he gave at Ottawa's Soft Rock Café, of all places, during a farewell party for Manning at the time he left the House of Commons.

There was every sign of the strong mutual respect the two men had for each other, which dated back to the late sixties. It began when, at the behest of Ernest Manning, Preston's father, and Peter Lougheed, the new leader of the Alberta Tories, they took on the task of seeing if provincial Socreds and Tories could be brought together.

In brief, Clark spoke both of Manning's legacy and his future. His legacy, he said, was that he had changed the face of Canadian politics; his future was that there was still much for him to do in his new role as a "scout" for the Canadian political centre-right. Clark spoke in a way that communicated his own willingness to keep two-way communication going.

Hearing those words and re-echoing them through my mind a few days later, when reading a piece by veteran columnist William Johnson, created some more of that outside-the-box, small-c Christian analysis that has seeped its way through this book.

"Doing politics christianly..." #67 was written on March 27, 2002.

WHEN IS A LIBERAL NOT A LIBERAL?

If you can't beat 'em, get some of 'em to join you.

That deceptively simple concept is embedded in a column that William Johnson wrote in The Globe and Mail *on March 14, 2002. Entitled "Old blueprint for a new realignment," Johnson's piece reaches back into the sixties for a thin tome penned by one Ernest Manning, who had just completed twenty-five years as Alberta's premier. Entitled* Political Realignment, *the book was allegedly ghostwritten by Manning's son, Preston.*

Its major thesis — in Johnson's crisply distilled phraseology — was "a political realignment by a party proposing a clear right-wing ideology of individualism as opposed to collectivism, economic freedom rather than regimentation, the family and voluntary associations rather than the state as the prime agents of social responsibility.

"And as the condition for everything else, fiscal responsibility. It implies clear lines of jurisdiction between federal and provincial governments."

And who did these proponents of realignment envisage as the stewards of such an arrangement? Well, the Progressive Conservative party, reconstituted to encompass ideological conservatives of all parties, including the Liberals (emphasis mine).

That hoary chestnut became, in fact, the harbinger of the Mulroney regime. Political Realignment *was written in 1967, not long before an almost-forgotten Robert Thompson rolled the old national Social Credit party into the Tories, twelve years before Joe Clark formed a minority government after defeating the mighty Pierre Trudeau only to give the crown back to the Liberals seven months later. More significantly, perhaps, it was sixteen years before Brian Mulroney won the first of two massive majorities in the House of Commons — larger than either Trudeau or Chrétien have ever been able to achieve. Check the history. Mulroney made political realignment work for a few years at least.*

Now, Thompson was a praying man. Interestingly, he prayed more comfortably with Liberal Prime Minister Lester Pearson than with his Conservative predecessor John Diefenbaker, who was, most of the time, a staunch Baptist. But when it came to rolling over the Social Credit party, he chose the Conservatives, not the Liberals.

There are some historic reasons for this.

It is current accepted intelligence that evangelical Christians park their vote with the Liberals in Ontario and the Alliance in the west. Furthermore, there are a fair number of Liberal MPs among those 100 or so from Ontario who, by faith culture, would be Alliance if they came from the west. I can recall that one Ontario pastor told me that any evangelical MPs who would be inclined to switch from Liberal to Alliance would be stupid to do so in the current atmosphere because they would erase their plurality in an instant with the Ontario centre-right vote split.

Over against that is the occasional tongue-in-cheek suggestion that someone like John Manley or Paul Martin could, given time and space, leave the Liberals and join up with a centre-right amalgam, perhaps taking the country with them. Political analyst Peter C. Newman actually made that suggestion, at least half seriously, with respect to Paul Martin at the time the United Alternative was grinding its way through to forming the CA.

Now, my quick take on either Martin or Manley moving to such a position and succeeding is that it's about as likely as 100 monkeys pecking out all the works of Shakespeare on 100 PCs, given a deadline of 100 years. But that is today. What would be needed to create a real realignment is enough togetherness on the right and centre to attract both conservative Liberals and some of their leaders.

However, the conservative types in the conservative parties, especially those whose conservatism grows out of their faith, will need to be smart enough and open enough to recognize the Liberals who are really conservatives but who are under the big L for political survival purposes.

Wilson's scenario, written seven days before the CA leadership contest results were in, saw Stephen Harper and Joe Clark as the leaders into realignment. He wrote, "The best hope for a realignment on policy as envisaged by Ernest Manning is for Stephen Harper to lead the Alliance while Clark continues to lead the Conservatives. Harper could attract disenchanted Liberals and Tories from across the country. The fusion of parties could come later, perhaps after the next election."

He might be right. Yet, I can see a few other names in the cluster as necessary to give bulk to the prospect. Some could join Clark in senior statespersons' roles – Preston Manning, Deborah Grey and Paul Martin, for example. Could it be that one of those would become the leader of a reconstituted senate – an as-yet-undeveloped job description?

Others would be in Harper's corner or perhaps even his potential competitors for the prime ministerial mantle:

Diane Ablonczy, Chuck Strahl, Peter MacKay and John Manley, to cite a few.

Age and timing are as much factors in the emerging of any scenario as is political or social philosophy. It would be interesting to do a construct on the left side of the political spectrum, with the influence of the Christian left as a factor as well. Indeed, Political Realignment made the point that opposite the united right would likely be a united left, consisting of bright red Tories, left-Liberals and the NDP.

But that is something to talk about another day.

In retrospect, some facets of the political realignment story turn out differently in practice than were envisaged in political theory.

The epilogue walks us through some of those conundrums.

Epilogue

To this point, our consideration of the many places and ways where God's faithfulness and the faithfulness of those who name God's name are evident ended not long before the June 28, 2004, federal election. We have created scenarios and asked questions that could only find either their fulfillments or answers in and after that election.

I have chosen three "OttawaWatch" pieces to "put a wrap" on this book. One was written before the election but after the merger of the Canadian Alliance and Progressive Conservative parties and their confirmation of Stephen Harper as their new leader. The second came after the re-election of the Liberals as a minority government. The third particularly focuses on the same-sex marriage debate, which brought faith issues to the fore during the winter and into the spring of 2005.

In February 2004, five months before the federal election, I wrote about Deb Grey and David Kilgour. Both represented Edmonton ridings and both had been consistently Christian in the way they did politics. Grey announced that she was stepping down after close to fifteen years in the house. Kilgour had just been dropped from cabinet. Their decisions were pivotal to their long political careers. Here is what I wrote at the time.

Lloyd Mackey

New paths to walk for Grey and Kilgour

Changes are likely just ahead for two members of Parliament whose faith and political walks have been marked with diligence and integrity.

True, David Kilgour and Deborah Grey do not seem to have landed on their political feet in the manner of their Edmonton colleague Anne McLellan, who is now the powerful deputy prime minister in Paul Martin's new cabinet. Grey has been in the House of Commons for over a decade. She was the first Reformer, four years ahead of the fifty-two-member "class of '93." She had a stint as interim opposition leadership between the tenures of Preston Manning and Stockwell Day.

Kilgour has been in the House since 1979. He sat first with the Tories, then broke with Mulroney over the GST. In due course, he joined the Liberal benches.

Whatever else they are, both Kilgour and Grey are serious Christian believers. Several times, recently, they have addressed Christian groups together about their common and contrasting faith stances. Grey is relatively blunt-spoken; Kilgour leans toward diplomacy. Their styles match the roles they have played in the House of Commons. Grey, on the opposition side, has been required to ask hard-hitting questions of the government. Kilgour has served diplomatic cabinet posts, first as secretary of state for foreign affairs for Latin America and Africa and second for Asia and the Pacific. So careful nuancing, drawn on his background as a constitutional lawyer, has been his forte.

Grey's faith grew, in part, out of despair over an abusive father. When someone told her that Jesus loved her, she accepted that love with youthful verve. (In time, she happily reports, she and her father were reconciled.) In later years, she shared her faith musically in a Christian gospel singing group. Her education, in preparation for teaching high-school English, took place at Trinity Western and the University of Alberta. Her entry into politics began with a seemingly chance airport encounter with Gordon Shaw, an early Reform organizer. He challenged her to consider running. She did, winning a by-election in Beaver River, Alberta, in 1989.

Grey has often demonstrated tough love, most particularly when she broke with fellow Christian believer Stockwell Day, telling him, "Stock, there is no shame in admitting that you are not a leader."

She is happy, today, to opine that Day is a good foreign affairs critic and that the coming together of Canada's two conservative parties is a fine thing. She leaves politics with a strong sense that her future is in God's hands. And she looks forward to miles of biking with husband Lew on their twin Harleys.

For Kilgour, all the diplomacy in the world did not rescue him from the pitfalls of the current same-sex marriage debate. Explaining his missed vote on the issue, Kilgour told an Edmonton journalist that he was concerned that badly written law vis-à-vis marriage could lead to the legalization of such "unusualities" (my word, not his) as polygamy.

He exhibits no bitterness at being excluded from Paul Martin's cabinet, taking comfort in the PM's appointment of thirteen pro-traditional-marriage Liberals to cabinet or parliamentary secretary posts.

Throughout his career, Kilgour has often and consistently borne witness to his Christian faith — particularly to its ability to nurture reconciliation in an adversarial political system.

Lloyd Mackey

Is it time for him to return "home" to the Conservatives, now that their two segments have "reconciled"? He says no, admitting that many have asked him the same question. One senses that on that question, he will seek the advice of both his constituents and his conscience.

Grey has since written her memoirs, *Never Retreat, Never Explain, Never Apologize: My Life in Politics* (Key Porter, 2004).

Kilgour, though stripped of his cabinet status, continued to retain just about as much influence as he had before. After telling him he would have to move his office to a smaller, more remote location, the powers that be let him stay. More significantly, perhaps, has been the way in which he has been able to lever his role as chair of the Foreign Affairs subcommittee on human rights. He has made it into a useful tool to expose religious persecution and other human rights violations in many of the hot spot nations in Africa and Asia.

And, while he stayed with the Liberals for the 2004 election, only going independent in the spring of 2005, I am sure that his whole story has not yet been told.

One of the first major events in Ottawa after that 2004 election was the First Ministers meeting on health. As it turned out, the event revealed a fair amount about how power, ideas and policy might be brokered in the new minority parliament. The following was written October 14, 2004, in the week the meeting took place.

SOME SIMPLE RULES ABOUT CATCHING ELEPHANTS

Private delivery of health care was the "elephant in the room" about which no one wanted to talk at the First Ministers meeting in Ottawa that has been convening this

230

week. NDP leader Jack Layton used the elephant analogy in speaking the unspeakable.

Layton was, according to National Post *reporter Bill Curry, one of the opposition politicians sitting in the conference room, observing the premiers and prime minister tackle the health care agenda. The others were Conservative leader Stephen Harper and his health critic Steven Fletcher, NDP deputy leader Bill Blaikie and Bloc Québecois MP Stephane Bergeron.*

That bit of name-dropping helps to put into context a previous significant — and unprecedented — nationally-televised session. It was the September 9 press conference involving the three opposition leaders proposing unity of a sort in the new minority parliament.

At that session, Stephen Harper, flanked by Layton and Bloc leader Gilles Duceppe, proposed ways in which the opposition could advance process in the minority house, even while disagreeing on policy. The performance of the three was so smooth and professional that one of my press gallery colleagues half-seriously described it as a "bloodless coup." And therein is the significance of Layton's elephant reference.

When Layton speaks about private health care, he thunders his opposition to the concept. At the same time, he invariably nuances his attack by talking about "private for-profit" health care. Whether he realizes it or not, by so speaking he is making the elephant visible. Further, he is making it possible for the combined opposition to help the Liberals, ideologically surrounded, to admit that the elephant exists and, properly cared for, the beast will do more good than harm.

Pure Conservative ideology may arguably insist that private health care should be for profit. But the practical conservative will allow that half a loaf is a fair option. That means handling private health care in a way that service cuts a motivating swath down the middle. Such servant-hood sidesteps the harmful aspects of both a bureaucratic command system and the exploiting of health care for reasons of unvarnished profit.

For decades, non-profit private organizations – many of them religiously motivated – have handled health care effectively. In more recent times, those organizations have often partnered with public institutions. They did so in a way that preserved the faith-based values of the original sponsors but permitted the fiscal and technological critical masses required of an increasingly complex system.

Conservatives who take an incremental approach can usually live with this non-profit private approach. They are not bound to the concept that, for example, the only way to get new hospitals or more MRIs is to form companies, sell shares, trade on the TSX and otherwise work the market to redundancy.

Social democrats – and social gospellers, for that matter – are not necessarily bound to the assumption that the only properly motivated health care workers are those who are on public payroll.

There was no way that the politically and geographically eclectic group of individuals that formed the First Ministers meeting would be able to come to immediate conclusions about the private health care elephant. That does not make the animal any less non-existent. People of faith and of the book, both those who are politicians and those whom they serve, can help catch and domesticate this seemingly illusive leviathan.

It has always intrigued me that healthy churches and religious organizations contribute significantly to good health care. That First Ministers meeting provided some interesting fodder for my assumptions.

At the time of writing, the same-sex marriage debate — or, at least, the 2005 version of it — was well underway. The Supreme Court of Canada's reference, released on December 9, 2004, paved the way for the government to introduce legislation, which it did on February 1.

Same-sex continuum continues

In issuing its response to the federal government's reference on same-sex marriage, the Supreme Court of Canada has created enough ambiguity to allow all sides to claim victory — and vow to continue the fight.

That fight has already started. Two of the protagonists, Canadians for Equal Marriage and Canada Family Action Coalition, have followed an old football truism: the best defense is a strong offence. The line of offence is the contention that the "other" side has "lots of money and will win if we don't fight." The corollary is "we are the underdogs, so if you are on our side, please join us in the fight."

A check of the Web sites for both above-mentioned organizations will confirm the similarity of strategies.

In between, there are several other advocacy groups and emerging think-tanks ready to weigh in with a range of nuances as to how to conduct the fight. And the politicians seem intent, already, to make this a real debate that ends up satisfying everyone to some extent but no one in totality.

In the early stages of the post-reference same-sex marriage debate, politicians all along the continuum have been positioning themselves to form coalitions around various parts of the issue.

John McKay, parliamentary secretary to the minister of finance, thought that he might have to vote in favour of same-sex marriage after learning that the Liberals planned a "two-line whip" on the vote. McKay has staked out his position as favouring traditional marriage by writing a chapter in Divorcing Marriage: Unveiling the Dangers in Canada's New Social Experiment *(Douglas Farrow and Daniel Cere, eds., McGill-Queen's University Press, 2004). The book and its authors are getting fair attention in some of the seemingly elitist eastern media because they address the issues with academic understatement rather than aggressive advocacy.*

When McKay found out about the two-line whip, which would have required parliamentary secretaries as well as cabinet ministers to vote with the government on the marriage issue, he had a little conversation with the prime minister. So did a few other parliamentary secretaries. The result: a one-line whip. Only cabinet ministers have to toe the mark.

McKay went one step further. He went public with the view that Paul Martin ought to free up the cabinet for the vote, too. The wrinkle, of course, was that when Paul Martin appointed his cabinet after assuming office a year ago, he took thirteen people into cabinet or parliamentary secretary roles who had voted, a few months before, in favour of male–female marriage. The numbers changed little after last June's election.

McKay favours what are described as "across-the-board" civil unions. That approach calls for the government to opt out of defining marriage, restoring the institution to its sometime role as a mainly religious celebration. These unions have been advocated by those such as John Redekop, retired political science professor and former chair of the

Evangelical Fellowship of Canada, and Margaret Somerville, a Catholic ethicist and law professor at McGill. The main argument in its favour is that, on first glance, it removes the equality argument long advanced by gay activists – the suggestion that rights equal to marriage are not enough; the use of the "M-word" must be granted as well.

After all, if equality works one way, it should work the other, the across-the-boarders contend.

John Reynolds, house leader at the time for the Conservative party, took up the cudgels for across-the-board civil unions on December 12 during CTV's "Question Period."

In so doing, he was reflecting the thinking of a number of Conservatives who view themselves as both Christian and libertarian. They have no difficulty in personally defining marriage as between a man and a woman, but support the state's right to disentangle itself from what they see to be an essentially religious issue.

However, two days later, Conservative leader Stephen Harper proposed three amendments for whatever same-sex marriage bill the Liberals bring forward. The Tories' thrust is to:

- *Retain the male–female marriage definition.*
- *Provide equality with marriage, in terms of legality and benefits, for other types of unions.*
- *Specifically protect religious organizations from, for example, being denied charitable status for declining to solemnize same-sex unions.*

Harper noted that he had strong caucus support for that approach, which means that, for now, Reynolds must be presumed to be in the minority. The Conservative leader is staking that stance on the argument that simply declaring traditional marriages and same-sex unions as equal before the law will meet the Charter's equality standard.

Back to the Liberal side. A little dust-up developed this week from the comments on CPAC (the parliamentary access channel) coming from Mauril Belanger, minister of democratic reform. Belanger suggested, on CPAC, that those marriage commissioners who want to opt out of performing same-sex marriages on conscience or religious grounds should be fired. Several Conservatives climbed all over Belanger, but received their responses from Justice Minister Irwin Cotler, who insisted that the Charter references to religious officials include public officials who are religious. Later, following the December 14 question period, Cotler had a "clarification briefing" in which he suggested that the feds don't have all the say with respect to provincially-appointed marriage commissioners.

To people who bring up quotes such as Belanger's, Cotler promises that he will sit down with his provincial counterparts, especially those countenancing the firing of religiously-motivated commissioners, and try to explain the Charter to them.

Cotler loves explaining things. He is known sometimes to seemingly mistake his opposite number, Conservative justice critic Vic Toews, for a student back in his university classroom. His lecturing demeanor toward Toews does not serve him well. They both have outstanding legal minds, and, in the best of circumstances, their debate on matters of justice and the law is a credit to the House of Commons.

Our last story today concerns NDP deputy house leader Bill Blaikie, a United Church minister. Just a few days before the release of the Supreme Court reference, he was interviewed on "Spirit Connection," a United Church Sunday night magazine show on Vision-TV.

Asked what sort of shift in emphasis he would like to see in his church, Blaikie expressed frustration at the amount of time spent in denominational circles on the same-sex issue. Not that he would castigate church leaders for their openness to pastoring gay and lesbian people. But he would like to see more church emphasis on long-standing social gospel issues, such as the alleviation of poverty, social justice, health and education.

Blaikie, Reynolds, Cotler, Belanger, Harper, McKay and Martin can each can be pinpointed at a different place along the same-sex marriage continuum. For that reason, the debate on whatever legislation the government puts forward will include discussion of some complex issues.

I will risk four predictions.

- *Some pundits are predicting that Cotler would like to have the bill wrapped up by April 2, the twenty-second anniversary of the instituting of the Charter of Rights and Freedoms. I would suggest that the complexities of the continuum will cause the debate to continue much longer.*

- *The minority situation may bring success for some opposition amendments, but they might not be those listed above. A fair amount of arm wrestling may occur in all parties, but I would suggest that, come what may, the across-the-board civil union idea may carry the day.*

- *No matter the outcome, the battle on same-sex relationships will be stepped up in the churches, even as it winds down on the state scene. Religious freedom will be attacked, not so much by politicians and government bureaucrats as by gay activists who are working for change in their own denominations.*

- *Over against that, there will be many gay and lesbian churchgoers who will not press for change, as*

*long as they receive warm pastoral care and encour-
agement for the particular gifts they bring to the
Christian community. They have no more interest
in politicizing such issues than most of their heterosexual friends who make up over ninety-five percent
of the congregations of which they are part.*

THE STORY CONTINUES

Because the faith-based stories from the Ottawa political arena all continue, I can safely say that the end of this
book is not the end. In fact, now that I have retired from
active Christian newspaper management, I am able to
spend a fair amount of time in the Parliamentary Press
Gallery. Out of that turn of events has come the possibility
of spending more time on Ottawa*Watch*, a weekly news and
analysis service designed especially for Christian leaders,
communicators and influencers. This service is freely available on two Web sites: www.canadianchristianity.com and
www.christiancurrent.com.

Ottawa*Watch* is undergirded by a number of Canadian
Christians who see the service as helpful to Christian
leaders who want to bring biblical concepts to bear on
public policy issues. This support base has been developed through Christian Info Canada, a federally-incorpo-
rate registered charity through which a good deal of
Christian information and newspaper development work
has been taking place over the past quarter-century.

Readers of this book who want to add their support for
this ministry can write to Christian Info Canada through
lmackey@christiancurrent.com for details. You will receive a
letter from John Irwin, the CIC board chair, that will

explain how such support can be arranged. The strength of Ottawa*Watch* is that it can be both non-advocacy and non-partisan. It is, in effect, point-of-view journalism — though the point of view is not so much the writer's opinion but, rather, the point from which he views the political scene, the press gallery in Ottawa.

Readers of this book and of Ottawa*Watch* may or may not agree with the writer. That is not quite the point. Rather, it is to be able to see politics and issues through the eyes of the writer and use the analysis in formulating one's own decisions about how to engage the political process.

By God's grace, I hope to be in and around Parliament Hill for another three years at least, to cover the continuing story of the faith/politics interface.

April 15, 2005